No easy walk

► ► ►

► ► ► In the Visual Studies series, edited by Douglas Harper

Also in the series:

Ronald Silvers, *A Pause on the Path* (1988)

Builder Levy, *Images of Appalachian Coalfields* (1989)

Richard Quinney, *Journey to a Far Place: Autobiographical Reflections* (1991)

Glenn Busch, *You Are My Darling Zita* (1991)

Melody D. Davis, *The Male Nude in Contemporary Photography* (1991)

David Heiden, *Dust to Dust: A Doctor's View of Famine in Africa* (1992)

Charles Keil, Angeliki V. Keil, and Dick Blau, *Polka Happiness* (1992)

Helen M. Stummer   *No easy walk* ▸▸▸

Newark, 1980–1993

Temple University Press
Philadelphia

Temple University Press, Philadelphia 19122
Copyright © 1994 by Temple University. All rights reserved
Published 1994
Printed in the United States of America

The paper used in this publication meets the minimum requirements of American
National Standard for Information Sciences—Permanence of Paper for Printed
Library Materials,
ANSI Z39.48–1984 ⊚

Library of Congress Cataloging-in-Publication Data
Stummer, Helen M., 1936–
       No easy walk : Newark, 1980–1993 / Helen M. Stummer.
            p. cm.—(Visual studies)
       ISBN 1-56639-242-X (alk. paper).—ISBN 1-56639-243-8 (pbk. :
alk. paper)
       1. Afro-Americans—New Jersey—Newark—Pictorial works. 2. Poor—New
Jersey—Newark—Pictorial works. 3. Newark (N.J.)—Social conditions—
Pictorial works. 4. Documentary photography—New Jersey—Newark. I. Title.
II. Series.
F144.N69N46   1994
974.9′3200496073–dc20

                                                                        94-6476

To my dear husband, Douglas W. Tatton, ▶ ▶ ▶

who helped make my dream a reality

▲
▲ ▲

Carol, December 1986

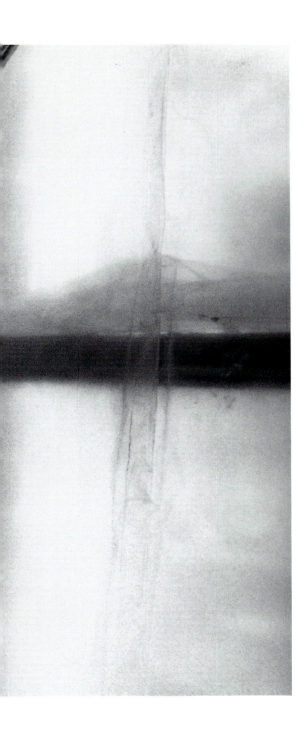

There were two things I wanted to do. ▶ ▶ ▶

I wanted to show the things that had

to be corrected. I wanted to show the

things that had to be appreciated.

—Lewis Hine

Contents

▶ ▶ ▶

I am deeply grateful to the people of Newark who allowed me into their lives, shared their stories, and gave me permission to photograph them. I also owe thanks to many who have given me moral support and encouragement throughout this project.

A number of people read the manuscript and gave me their valued opinions: Gwen Dungy, Dean of Arts and Humanities at the County College of Morris; William Linder, founder of New Communities; Karen Olson, founder of Interfaith Hospitality; Lynn Waiters, of the Newark Public Advocates Office; William Dane, Keeper for Special Prints, Newark Library; Susan Perger and Anne Prucha, of Legal Services, New Brunswick; Beverly Lowy, editor; Clarence Williams, sociologist; Gretchen Ney, artist.

I thank Charles Cummings, official Newark historian and Associate Director for Special Collections, Newark Library, for going over the Introduction for accuracy with a fine-tooth comb. My appreciation also goes to the reference librarians of the New Jersey section of the Newark Public Library for their cooperation, and to Pat Thomas-Cappello, Bonnie Franklin, and Ann Mathious of the Grants Office of CCM (County College of Morris) for their important assistance in obtaining and administering grants from the CCM and the Geraldine R. Dodge Foundations.

This book was a collaboration between Carol, Jane Peterson, and me. Throughout these many years, Carol's patience with my endless questions and photographing were a documenter's dream. She believed even more than I that this book would someday be published. And in discouraging times, it was her words and spirit that helped me through.

My sincere appreciation is extended to the New Jersey Historical Commission and the Mid-Atlantic Arts Foundation. With their aid I was able to engage Jane Peterson, a professional writer and editor, who developed a concept for the book from my mountains of papers and photographs. Through many long work sessions, she encouraged me to dig deeper and deeper into my memory, always being sensitive to the need to keep the writing in my own voice. After writing each

Acknowledgments

▶ ▶ ▶

story, we would go over it again and again and again. The introductory chapter was the most challenging section. It was important to give historical context to the experiences of immigrant and southern migrant families, mine and Carol's among them, who came to Newark looking for a better life. Jane's professionalism and her personal support are also appreciated.

In addition, I thank the people at Temple University Press for their belief in the message of this book and their willingness to make it available to a wide audience.

The title is taken from *No Easy Walk to Freedom* (1965), a collection of writings and speeches by Nelson Mandela.

This book documents the survival struggles of some of the poorest people in Newark, New Jersey—residents of the Central Ward—who balance precariously on the edge of homelessness, a paycheck or welfare check away from the street. Many of the people I came to know live on Irvine Turner Boulevard, once Belmont Avenue, where the rebellion of 1967 began.

Most of the photographs I have taken on this street over the past ten years portray African Americans whose struggles in the Central Ward are similar to the struggles of poor people of all races in most American cities, except that blacks have always been more discriminated against than any other group. But all strain to find housing and work in areas where both are scarce, to piece together a decent education where quality is low, to find physical security in an environment where little exists. So this book explores, more than anything else, how being poor affects daily life and how poor people understand their experience.

To visit the Central Ward each week, I cross between two jarringly different worlds. Although they live only a few miles away, the people in the suburban, middle-class town where I live and in the middle- and upper-class communities where I teach are generally ignorant about life in the inner city. My photographs and interviews are my way of trying to carry back to my world some understanding of poverty. But documentary photography not only shows outsiders what is happening to people around them; it can also be a vehicle for the subjects to reflect on their own experience. For example, Carol, on whom this book focuses, told me that after reading the manuscript and looking at my photographs, she felt that being poor and living in this situation wasn't all her own fault. In the course of this project, I have given pictures to almost everyone I have worked with, and the photographs have become parts of family history, marking milestones and documenting neighborhood change.

Although I discuss some of the reasons for Newark's general decline, my approach is largely personal. I have attempted to find out what it is like to be poor in the richest country in the world by entering people's lives and listening to their stories in these "bad neighborhoods."

After three years of photographing around the Central Ward, often with the help of a neighborhood improvement organization, I had the good fortune to meet Carol, a twenty-four-year-old mother of three. Gradually, she and her friend Rasheek took me under their wing, introducing me to friends and neighbors and shielding me from danger. Carol is perceptive, observant, and accurate. She has an uncanny ability to recount in detail what she sees and hears. Visiting once or twice a week, I spent hours photographing her and her family, friends, and neighbors and learning about their lives.

Carol's apartment is always full of people, many of whom she has helped—sometimes with advice, other times with food, clothes, and furniture that suburbanites have given me to take to Newark. Hugs and words of comfort are given freely, and many children have found support in Carol's mothering.

Because I used a variety of methods in reporting dialogue, there are some voice changes in the book. At times I used a tape recorder and transcribed the tapes verbatim. Other times I recalled a story and asked the person if it was accurate. Or I might have felt an anecdote was so significant that I asked the person to repeat it while I wrote it down. There were also occasions when I asked a person to elaborate on an event described to me years earlier.

In many ways, my journey into ghettos seems like a series of accidents. I never had a plan. The choices were mostly dictated by my heart rather than my head. I dropped out of school at sixteen, never thinking it would be possible to go back. But one day eleven years later I walked into the apartment of a new acquaintance, a Cooper Union graduate named Carole Wong Chesek, and everything changed. First a pottery jar full of artist's brushes and pencils on a picnic table caught my eye, then a row of books, and, on the walls beyond, beautiful maps. I was entranced. I had never seen anything like it. We talked for hours over jasmine tea, and for the first time in my life I felt that someone understood what I was trying to say. Later, with her encouragement, I bought my first book and then others, started to draw and paint, and began going to museums and concerts.

Suddenly, without planning, my life was on a different course. By the time I was thirty-four, and my children were still growing up, I got my general equivalency diploma (G.E.D.). Then I went on to Kean College, where, seven years later, I earned a B.A. (cum laude). At fifty, I earned an M.A. from Vermont College.

During my undergraduate years I happened upon an exhibit at the International Center of Photography in New York City that inspired me to sign up for a beginner's class. I wanted to learn how to use my camera better so I could take pictures of things that I wanted to paint. The instructor, Patt Blue, assigned each student to pick an area to document. No matter where I went, nothing seemed interesting. Patt, who had observed that photographing children was my strength, suggested that I practice photographing children at the Children's Aid Society on East Sixth Street, on the Lower East Side of Manhattan; and so my involvement with photography began.

I was terrified from the start. I feared unfamiliar places. Even going to college was an ordeal. For years, each time I entered a classroom I would break out in a cold sweat; I never raised my hand, never volunteered an answer or talked to a stranger. For the longest time while I was on Sixth Street all my negatives were blurry and I couldn't figure out why. Then one day, as I was getting ready to take a picture, I happened to notice that my hands were trembling violently. It was easy to solve this problem by just turning up the shutter speed. Other fears were less easy to overcome. With good reason, the *New York Times* called Sixth Street "the meanest street in America" in 1981.

My own childhood had been rough, but not like this, with people knifing each other. Fortunately for me, people on Sixth Street often took the trouble to teach me how to be street wise, how to survive in the ghetto. "Always watch out for falling debris being thrown from the rooftops," some warned. They explained that each street is different. "On this one you have to stick close to the buildings because people shoot at the other side from windows overhead." On another street, "You'd better walk near the curb so no one standing in a doorway can pull you in."

Luckily, I already had some street smarts. I had belonged to a gang as a young teenager. We got our thrills and bad reputation by dressing in black, smoking cigarettes, and standing on the corner looking mean. The biggest kick came when adults would cross the street to avoid us. That gave us the greatest sense of power. It also gave me a lifelong understanding of youngsters who dress differently—I know they are trying to act tough because they feel so powerless.

Being able to see through a tough facade also protected me from being easily intimidated. On the street, I knew it was important to make friends with the leaders, to seek out the toughest people on the block, explain what I was trying to do, and try to include them in my work. I also developed a strategy for dealing with anyone who looked menacing. If a man had a threatening look in his eye, normally I would have avoided that person and possibly crossed the street, but now I would go up to him and ask if he knew anyone in the photographs I always carried with me. Then I would ask if I could take his picture. Always, I returned the following week with a print and often I gained a friend.

The first day I began taking pictures on East Sixth Street, I had a blinding headache and could hardly focus. I kept repeating to myself something that I had read: "If you don't take risks, you will never do anything meaningful." Finally I saw a group of children playing around their mothers, who were sitting on a stoop. No one spoke English very well, so I pointed to my camera and then to the children. The mothers nodded their permission for me to take some pictures, and I did. I tried to tell them that I would return in a week with the photographs.

To my dismay, when I brought the photographs back, the mothers acted as though they had never seen me before. They didn't respond to the pictures of their children; their faces were utterly blank. As I stood there wondering about this odd situation, I heard some youngsters speaking English and asked them to find out why the mothers didn't want the photographs. "No dinero! No dinero!" the mothers said. "We have no money." "They're free, the pictures are free," I explained. Suddenly, the entire scene changed. Everyone began passing the photographs around, gesturing, and laughing over them. I spent the afternoon drinking coffee with the mothers and taking more photographs. And the following week I returned with the prints.

Each week in the car, driving to Manhattan from New Jersey, I would repeat my mantra and do deep-breathing exercises in order to manage my anxiety. When I arrived, the children would reassure me by running up to the car shouting my name and yelling, "Take me a picture! Take me a picture!" Their noisy reception made me feel safe and welcome, as though I belonged. This acceptance was especially comforting when I looked at the grim-faced men standing silently in doorways.

The process of returning each week and giving out photographs continued through the summer and into the fall. When the cold weather began, everyone went inside, and I knew that if I wanted to continue I would have to take more risks; walk up the narrow, dark stairway, knock on the door, and wait to see if someone would let me in. So, with pounding heart, one day I climbed the stairs, the door opened, and to my great relief the family behind it greeted me warmly. Once inside, I no longer felt shy. I then spent the winter photographing this family and listening to them tell stories about their struggles.

Of course, unlike the people I was photographing, I had choices. I had a safe place to go home to every night. In the ghetto, however, everyone is afraid all the time—there is no letup. One woman told me how people in this area have learned to "size up" a person in a matter of seconds, a skill fundamental to their survival. In any case, I was very glad they didn't peg me as an enemy.

Years later, when I asked a woman living on Sixth Street why I had encountered so few problems, she replied, "Most people thought you had to be crazy, so they left you alone. No normal person would walk along these streets loaded down with camera equipment the way you did. And if you wasn't crazy, then you certainly had to be a nun."

I continued working on East Sixth Street for five years. I never thought much about what I was doing or why. I just knew the minute I saw the street I had to photograph it. My way of going about it was also intuitive. It was natural to explain my purpose to the people I wanted to photograph—I wanted to show outsiders what it was like to live in this environment. Then, intruding as little as possible, I would watch and listen, waiting for the "right" composition or expression. Somehow those who accepted me sensed that I did not judge them for having little or no furniture and lots of roaches and rats, that I did not blame them for their situation. And the more they talked, the more apparent the injustice of their circumstances became. I grew more and more obsessed with showing their side of living in this environment.

In addition to giving me a feeling of belonging, photographing on Sixth Street gave me a sense of purpose. Tenants showed my pictures of broken pipes, falling ceilings, and dangling electrical wires to the violations bureau, and the violations were fixed. Sometimes just showing the photographs to the landlord got the job done. Less dramatically, my photographs often brought pleasure to families and their children.

On a personal level, it gradually became obvious that photography enabled me to express my feelings in ways that painting had not. Painting was completely solitary. Photography allowed me to interact with people and still be alone in the darkroom.

A 1972 photography exhibit by Diane Arbus at the Museum of Modern Art had a powerful effect on me, enabling me to peer through the veneer of odd or different-looking people, through their heavy makeup and cold expressions, to see the loneliness and insecurity that lay beneath the facade. Whenever I saw people like this, I used to turn away, as it seemed impolite to stare at them, but Diane Arbus not only looked at them, she photographed them. Now, thanks to her,

I felt I had permission to look more closely at things that made me uncomfortable.

Amazingly, people's reactions to my photographs often supported my way of seeing things. And this confirmation had a powerful healing effect on me. In my own lower-middle-class family, economic survival wasn't seriously threatened, but there was poverty of the spirit. Everyone was preoccupied with her or his own struggles. And, like many, perhaps all, children to some degree, I felt overlooked. A relative who took care of me as I was growing up planted the idea that my way of seeing things was crazy, and that I must be crazy. No one in the family paid any attention to what I said.

In 1980, a fluke led me to my next project. While driving on a New Jersey highway, I made a wrong turn and ended up circling the Central Ward in Newark, the city in which I was born. I was unfamiliar with the city and amazed at what I saw. One building after the other was burned out, their scarred remains scattered over one empty lot after another. It struck me that I ought to be working here instead of on the Lower East Side.

Working as a photojournalist for a Newark newspaper seemed like a good way to get to take pictures in this area, so I applied for a job as a stringer. The editor liked my photographs but suggested I cover sports events instead. They didn't do many local stories, he said, "because the people here throw their mothers off rooftops." As if to confirm his attitude, as I was driving around Newark after the interview, a police car pulled me over and asked me if I was lost. "No," I answered. "Okay, but you know this is a dangerous area," the officer warned, adding that I'd be better off staying out of it.

The police were not exaggerating. The Central Ward was dangerous. But this is not the whole story. It was also rewarding, and the problems here were no different from those on the Lower East Side. For a while, I worked in both places. But during this time Sixth Street became even more violent, with drug dealers taking over in the building next to the one where I had spent most of my time. And one day in 1981 three men cornered me in a hallway on Sixth Street and asked why I was taking pictures. "I only take pictures of children," I kept repeating as I skipped from one foot to the other. "If we ever see you take that camera out again," said one, "it's over for you."

I took this threat seriously, photographing only inside after that, and I thought more about Newark. Why should I be driving so far when there is a similar situation closer to home? Still, it saddened me to realize that my work on the Lower East Side was coming to an end. I couldn't just leave. So I turned hundreds of negatives into slides and got permission to show them in a community center on Sixth Street. There were so many people jammed into the center that they had to leave the doors open. As people caught sight of pictures of family and friends who had either died or moved away, or children who had been little and were now grown, they screamed in sadness or delight.

In Newark, I worked as I did in Manhattan, giving out photographs and becoming involved. "Involved" is an important word. Actually, friends and relatives used to warn me about getting "too involved"—that people would take advantage of me and want to come home with me. But no one in the ghetto ever asked to come home with me; they liked their neighborhood because it was familiar and they were close to family and friends. What people really wanted was to have the neighborhood fixed up so they could find a decent place to live and, just as important, a decent place to work.

Though I do strive for balance and fairness, my passion to see change take place in communities like the Central Ward is evident. There is no escaping the conclusion that the wrenching social problems described in these pages need to be addressed. It is my hope that this book will help to change conventional beliefs about the causes of poverty and to correct the common assumption that poor people are to blame for their plight. Only then can we as a nation make affordable housing and employment a priority for local and federal government.

Introduction

The transformation of Newark

▶ ▶ ▶

Irving Turner Boulevard, March 1993. For ten years Carol lived in the building on the right, in the first-floor apartment (window showing). After that, for almost two years she lived in the basement apartment in the building on the left.

▼
▼
▼

For those of us who were born in Newark or simply spent time there before moving on to the suburbs, the riot in the summer of 1967 burned away our fond memories and remaining ties to the city; our lives became divided into "before" and "after" the riot. After the riot, the saying goes, Newark became "white by day, black by night"; despite a remarkable rebirth of the downtown area, and efforts to avoid its polarization, the city became steadily poorer. Many white suburbanites appear to hold the mostly African American residents of the city responsible for the decline of certain areas; in their view, the wonderful schools and neighborhoods have been run into the ground by blacks. Their own family histories seem to tell them that European immigrants faced the same hardships as black migrants but overcame them through hard work and sacrifice to fulfill the American dream. They assume that unemployed African Americans simply don't want to work.

Wanting to understand how these harsh beliefs came about and how the city had become so divided, I spent eleven years listening and talking to, photographing, and finally collaborating with Carol. She has helped me to understand the daily struggles of her family and neighbors, and together we have tried to make sense of our own diverging experiences.

Even though we are a generation apart in age, Carol and I discovered that our family histories had some common elements. Our maternal grandparents were the first in our families to uproot themselves—mine from Hungary in 1903, hers from West Virginia in 1948—and to move to Newark in search of work. By working hard, they supported their families fairly well. We wondered whether the city had offered them similar challenges and opportunities in finding work and a place to live. So we decided to ask our mothers what they knew about their families' reactions to the city. To learn more about the experiences of the early immigrants and African American migrants from the South, I did some research in the New Jersey section of the Newark Public Library.

I read that the early European immigrants had indeed been mistreated and terribly deprived in Newark. In the nineteenth century, Protestant Anglo-Saxon residents accepted Europeans as workers to help build the city and man its factories, but not as neighbors. Soon after Europeans began coming in large numbers, bitter antiforeign and especially anti-Catholic feeling erupted in violent attacks on property and individuals. Established groups in nineteenth-century American cities commonly blamed slum dwellers' "filthy habits" and deviation from "chaste," "pious," and "sober" behavior for the terrible conditions of their lives.[1] Then, as now, the well-to-do regarded the poor as threatening and kept them at a distance. And some nineteenth-century property deeds specifically prohibited sale to any negroes or natives of Ireland.[2]

Though large numbers of these immigrants failed or returned home, many more prospered; by the end of the nineteenth century people of Irish and German descent outnumbered Anglo-Saxons and gained some influence in the city.[3] Newark thrived. Its leaders greatly improved health conditions and built schools, parks, and rapid transit.

The newly successful immigrants generally treated newcomers from other countries as badly as they had been treated; but they welcomed their own countrymen and women, encouraging relatives to join them here. At the turn of the century the Irish were doing so well that many would no longer take menial jobs. A Newark contractor hiring a thousand laborers for the railroad at the time observed that "the man who comes over from Ireland now, as a rule, has friends here . . . and in nine cases out of ten his friends have taken care to provide him with work in a shop or some place where he can learn a trade and earn more money than he could as a laborer."[4] More recent arrivals, Italians and others, took those jobs and later moved up in much the same way as the Irish.

So when my Hungarian and German forebears arrived in Newark early in the twentieth century, they walked on roads smoothed by others before them. And, like many immigrants at this time, they had relatives and friends waiting to open doors to jobs and housing. At the

1. Charles Abrams, *The City Is the Frontier* (New York: Harper & Row, 1965), 20.

2. Kenneth T. Jackson, *Crabgrass Frontier: The Suburbanization of the United States* (New York: Oxford University Press, 1985), 76.

3. Kenneth T. Jackson and Barbara B. Jackson, "The Black Experience in Newark: The Growth of the Ghetto, 1870–1970," in *New Jersey Since 1860: New Findings and Interpretations,* ed. William C. Wright (Trenton: New Jersey Historical Commission, 1972), 42.

4. John T. Cunningham, *Newark* (Newark: New Jersey Historical Society, 1988), 202.

age of twenty, my maternal grandmother, for example, already had a job as a governess lined up when she left Budapest in 1903. And as soon as she arrived in Newark she went straight to a roominghouse on Raymond Boulevard that a friend had recommended.

Living in the same roominghouse was a man my grandmother had first met in a tea shop in Budapest. He believed that fate had brought them together. And, knowing that she was "the saving kind," he began giving her his pay each week. A year later, she married him, and although they never got along very well, the marriage was a financial success. For the rest of her life my grandmother served as a kind of bank for the family, lending money to my parents for our house, for example, and always collecting interest.

Unlike some of my other relatives, my maternal grandfather had come to Newark with no contacts, but he did have a skill. So he was able to answer an advertisement in a window for a part-time job fine-tuning machinery at the Singer Sewing Machine Company in Elizabeth, and he ended up working there for forty years.

When my father landed in Newark in 1910, he had people to go to, a sister and her husband, the prosperous editor of a German newspaper. My father was only seventeen at the time. Fortunately, his mother had insisted that he learn a skill before leaving Germany, and his brother-in-law got him a job refinishing pianos for the Lauda Piano Company. Before long, my father had saved enough money to bring over his father and brother.

Carol's African ancestors of course came to America long before my relatives, but not by choice. Wrenched from their families, they eventually formed new ones, but until the end of the Civil War African Americans never knew when their families might be broken up again, when a spouse or a child or parent would be sold to a distant owner. Some descendants of slaves have been able to trace their families far back, but Carol knows nothing about her ancestors beyond her grandparents, who moved to Newark after World War II.

At the time that my grandmother arrived in the city, in 1903, there were about six thousand African Americans living there, just under 3 percent of the population. At this time, relations between blacks and the foreigners and children of foreigners who made up three-fourths of the city's population were reasonably good. That is, in Newark there were few reported incidents of racial violence, unlike in the South, where blacks often feared for their lives. Living in small clusters among whites throughout much of the city, African Americans were scarcely noticed by the European American majority. My mother, for example, who is now eighty-four, lived in the Central Ward, or the Hill District (also known as the Third Ward), at the corner of Mercer and West from her birth in 1909 until 1921, and she says that she never saw a black person until she was twelve.

My research confirmed that nearly all African Americans in Newark worked in menial positions—the men as unskilled laborers, servants, draymen, and so forth, the women as laundresses and servants. Their job opportunities differed greatly from those of Europeans because a widespread policy among employers and trade unions kept them out of skilled positions. Many whites who believed that blacks were incapable of becoming skilled workers must have been ignorant of the presence of ironworkers, carpenters, stonemasons, brewers, and bricklayers among the slaves in New Jersey during colonial times and after independence.

In the library I found a government survey of New Jersey factories in 1903, in which a number of employers wrote that blacks were lazy and unreliable and "could not be trained to do the work." But some owners observed instead that their hesitation to hire blacks grew out of their workers' fear that blacks, who worked for lower wages, would replace them. And one manufacturer of tools and hardware stated that they employed no black workers because "we do not think our men would make it agreeable for them. This we believe to be the reason why negroes do not enter the field of skilled mechanics."[5]

On the other hand, black longshoremen reportedly feared they would lose their jobs if they joined a union because they believed "that if they demanded the same wage as white men, employers would prefer the latter, and that they should thereby loose [sic] the employment

5. Clement Alexander Price, *Freedom Not Far Distant: A Documentary History of Afro-Americans in New Jersey* (Newark: New Jersey Historical Society, 1980), 208.

entirely."[6] It seems that many workers, both union and nonunion, felt that their jobs were uncertain. Employers undoubtedly enjoyed having a large and growing pool of available workers, but the experienced workers were automatically at odds with newcomers.

A few trade unions admitted "negroes," but generally, skilled jobs and most municipal jobs—for firemen, policemen, and clerks, for example—would remain off-limits to blacks until the 1960s and 1970s.

In the library I also found interesting statistics showing that a few African Americans in Newark ran small businesses, and that in 1920 there were eleven black doctors and eight black nurses. Although the public schools were integrated in 1909, blacks, even those with college degrees, were not allowed to teach in them.[7] Difficult as these circumstances were, the African American community was strong, and many considered themselves fortunate to live in Newark at the turn of the century in what was known as its "golden age."

This relatively positive situation and the calm relations between the races eroded during World War I, when tens of thousands of new workers seeking jobs flooded Newark, a city of 347,469 in 1910.[8] Among them were thousands of black tenant farmers who had been recruited in Alabama and Georgia by agents working for manufacturers.[9] The sudden influx of poor people strained the relatively small city beyond its capacity. Between 1916 and 1919, Newark's expenses rose faster than the income, forcing the city to raise taxes. Many resident blacks resented the intrusion of southern migrants and worried that their own image would suffer as a result of being identified with country people unaccustomed to the ways of the city.

Then as now, the poor suffered from health problems at a far higher rate than those who were better off, and blacks, being among the poorest, were less healthy than whites, even those living in the same impoverished neighborhoods. In 1917 an observer described the "country people recently arrived from . . . Georgia and Alabama . . . crowded into dark rooms" with inadequate clothing and heat, shiv-

7 ▶ ▶ ▶

6. Ibid., 211.
7. Jackson and Jackson, "Black Experience," 44–45.
8. Price, *Freedom Not Far*, 14–15.
9. Cunningham, *Newark*, 252.

ering with the cold. "It is a small wonder," she noted, "that illness has overtaken large numbers."[10]

In 1919, tuberculosis in the Central Ward drove the black mortality rate up to more than three times the white rate in the same district. This severely crowded district, which had become nearly a third black by then, led the city in number of cases of meningitis, influenza, and pneumonia. Part of the problem was the lack of access to health care. Many doctors and hospitals would not take black patients.

It seems likely that poor health affected people's ability to show up for work or, if they did appear, to step as lively as the boss wanted them to. Conceivably, health problems and the southern way of talking and moving contributed to the image of poor blacks as slow and unreliable. But census information undermines such stereotypes; in 1930 proportionately more black than white workers over the age of fourteen were gainfully employed in Newark.[11] Through hard work, African Americans made small gains in business and the professions between 1910 and 1930. The numbers of black painters, carpenters, construction laborers, and mechanics grew. And the number of blacks in industry nearly doubled between 1920 and 1930, though nearly all were still stuck in menial jobs. During this period the black migrant population more than doubled, and as white anxieties increased, segregation became more rigid and widespread.

With the Great Depression in 1929, the town that had advertised itself as the "city of opportunity" saw more than a third of its factories close, six hundred in all. By 1931, roughly sixty thousand residents were out of work, almost a third of the city's workers. Fortunately for my grandparents, people needed sewing machines more than ever, and somehow the demand for pianos held up as well, so my father's business survived. But people without such luck were in serious trouble.

By 1938–1939, nearly twenty-four thousand people were on relief in the city. African Americans filled almost a third of the relief rolls, although they made up only one-eleventh of the population. Menial workers such as servants were the most expendable. The dis-

10. Price, *Freedom Not Far,* 215.

11. Jackson and Jackson, "Black Experience," 46.

proportionate numbers of blacks on relief may have contributed to the rumors that hordes of poor negroes were heading north to take advantage of relief services. A 1941 study established that all but 5 percent of black families on relief had moved to Newark before 1932, but people were either unaware of this information or unpersuaded, and they continued to repeat the false stories.[12]

World War II brought full employment to Newark, and once again black labor was needed for war production. President Franklin Roosevelt issued an executive order in 1941 prohibiting racial discrimination in defense work. In Newark, for the first time, several thousand blacks were hired for the full range of positions in a government office—the Office of Dependency Benefits (ODB)—and they performed well.[13] But with the war's end and the closing of the ODB, blacks lost jobs and the chance to demonstrate their competence. Although many individuals were worse off after the war, people were slow to recognize that the city was declining, that it was gradually losing its manufacturing base as well as its population. And blacks, Carol's maternal grandparents among them, continued to migrate to Newark in search of work. The fact that the city was still booming in some areas, and the continued presence of overt discrimination and danger in the South, continued to make Newark attractive to poor southerners. Carol's grandparents were unusually lucky in that they had jobs waiting when they moved to Newark in 1948.

Carol's grandfather had discovered at the age of fourteen that he loved to cook, and he served in the navy for many years, attaining the rank of chief petty officer. The job offer in Newark came from the former owner of the West Virginia bakery where Carol's grandfather had made very popular doughnuts from his own recipe. When he arrived in New Jersey, he discovered that his job depended on handing over the recipe; refusing to give up his secret, he found a job cooking in the Veterans' Administration (VA) hospital. Eventually he started his own business, the Sweet Shop, where he sold his famous doughnuts and home-cooked meals.

Like my father, Carol's grandfather was fortunate to have a skill

12. Ibid., 49.
13. Cunningham, *Newark*, 296–297.

that was in demand. In recent years, many menial jobs have been eliminated through automation, and many blue-collar jobs have moved overseas where labor costs are lower. Singer Sewing Machine Company, for example, where my grandfather worked, pulled up stakes in the United States fifteen years ago. White-collar jobs increased in Newark, which continued to be a financial and commercial center, but this expansion bypassed much of the local labor force, which was largely unskilled, attracting skilled workers from outside the city instead. From then on, there would be a mismatch between local jobs and workers.

With hindsight, it is easy to see that the problems with the job situation in Newark and other cities lay deeper and farther back than many people realized. Since the nineteenth century, employers had been moving outward in search of cheaper land and lower taxes. This drain accelerated after World War II. Between 1950 and 1970 about fifty-eight thousand manufacturing jobs left, just as thousands of southern blacks were streaming into the city in search of work and a better life for their children. To cope with the departure of employers to the suburbs, where blacks were rarely allowed to live, about half of Newark's black men and women commuted out of the city every day to work.

Newark is physically small—23.4 square miles—and since the late nineteenth century people have dealt with crowding by moving beyond the city limits. At first, only the well-to-do could afford to escape, but after 1910, middle-class people like my relatives began moving as well. By 1925, about 40 percent of the city's attorneys lived in the suburbs, and by 1932, fully 86 percent of the officers and board members of the chamber of commerce lived outside the city. My own parents left Newark in 1938 when my mother protested that their house was too small.

Traditionally, immigrants who succeeded worked their way up into better jobs. They saved enough money to buy a piece of real estate, which often grew in value, and later they bequeathed it to their children. Many moved just over the city line to escape the noises and smells of factories, to put distance between themselves and poor people, to gain privacy.

My relatives were among these lucky ones. One great-uncle made so much money selling glasses of beer and lunch for ten cents in his Down Neck tavern that he was able to buy three houses in Irvington as an investment. The brother-in-law who hosted my father during his first year in Newark owned an impressive detached house in Vailsburg. And in 1926, just sixteen years after he arrived in Newark, my father bought a house on South 20th Street. My maternal grandparents saved money partly by remaining in a cheap rental apartment in the Central Ward for seventeen years, and in 1921 they bought a big house in Maplewood, an attractive area on the outskirts of Newark.

African Americans did not make such quick progress on this route to a better life. Not only did they earn lower pay than whites but they also paid higher rents and were restricted to crowded areas with inferior housing. In 1917, after the workers recruited in the South had settled in Newark, an employee of the city sanitary division noted that "the white landlords take the opportunity of extorting high rents for miserable shacks, cellars and basements."[14] And forty years later, a study of slum rents in Newark found blacks still being charged substantially more than whites for comparable apartments.[15]

Even blacks who managed to accumulate savings ran into obstacles my relatives never encountered. Very few owners would sell to them, and financial institutions discriminated against them when they tried to get housing loans. The clauses in property deeds forbidding sale to the Irish had quietly disappeared, but those against "Negroes" held firm until the Supreme Court ruled against them in 1948, and they continued in effect for at least twenty years after that. African Americans sometimes got around such restrictions by paying a premium. Once they found a willing buyer, they could secure financing in "the gray market" outside of traditional banks and savings and loan associations. There must also have been some family financing, as there was between my parents and my grandmother, but since blacks generally could not accumulate as much wealth as whites, this option

14. Ibid., 252.
15. George Groh, *Profiles of a Ghetto* (New York: Weybright and Talley, 1972), 199.

was probably not widely available. So people filled in either by borrowing from high-priced lenders or by paying above-market prices to owners who would then finance their mortgages, often at higher rates. In this way, some blacks managed to move out of the worst slums into better parts of the city.

We are so familiar with the idea of public housing that I was surprised to learn that the government was not directly involved in shelter until the Great Depression, when construction nearly stopped altogether and almost half of all homeowners had lost or were close to losing their homes. With a thousand mortgages across the country being foreclosed every day at one point, and people being turned out onto the street, the federal government stepped in to tackle the emergency. A new agency, the Federal Housing Administration (FHA), was set up to insure mortgages, which took much of the risk out of lending, thereby encouraging banks and savings and loan associations to lend to more people. The FHA helped get the construction industry back on its feet and made it possible for millions of middle-class families to own homes.

The FHA also had an enormous impact on where Americans would live, the kinds of buildings they would live in, and who would or would not live next door. This shift came about in part through a new system for appraising buildings that was adopted by the FHA and, following its example, the banks and savings and loan associations it worked with.

The group that created the appraisal system believed that density, ethnic and racial mixing, income mixing, and old buildings were undesirable. In other words, city living was undesirable. Convinced that any one of these typically urban factors even in small quantities would depress property values, they discouraged investment in areas where even one of these elements was present. At the same time, they encouraged lending to buyers of new houses in low-density, homogeneous communities.

These FHA policies accelerated the departure of the white middle class from the cities to the suburbs. People like my father and Carol's grandfather, who loved Newark and didn't want to leave it, were not consulted by policymakers. Nor were the planners who doubted the wisdom of scattering human settlements over the countryside without considering the long-term social and economic impact of the automobile on which these settlements depended.

The assumptions of FHA standards were widely known and accepted without question as fact. I never heard my father make a racial slur, but I do remember his worried remark in 1957 when we put our house—we lived in Union then—on the market. He said he hoped no Negro would walk by when a potential buyer came. Ordinary people like my father had no information with which to challenge the belief that the presence of blacks depressed property values, a false idea that was constantly repeated in books and articles by experts. The FHA manual itself specifically warned against "infiltration of inharmonious racial and national groups."[16]

The FHA used appraisal methods based on color-coded Residential Security Maps—green, blue, yellow, and red—ranking new, homogeneous neighborhoods green, or first. Although any ethnic and racial mixing was considered bad, some groups supposedly hurt property values more than others. The presence of Jews would demote even the best neighborhood to blue or yellow, but black neighborhoods were colored red no matter what their condition. Although the maps were kept secret from the general public, they were available to banks and real estate interests.[17]

Records show that the entire city of Newark—old, largely working class, and mixed in race and ethnicity, not to mention income—was effectively branded a poor investment. Vailsburg and Forest Hill, as well as "high-class Jewish" sections such as Weequahic and Clinton Hill, received only blue, second-grade ratings; the well-maintained, working-class sections of Roseville, Woodside, and East Vailsburg were graded third, or yellow. The rest of the city, including the Ironbound district and the Central Ward, was rated last, as "hazardous," or red.[18]

It seems a hazardous rating generally became a self-fulfilling

16. Abrams, *The City*, 61.

17. Jackson, *Crabgrass Frontier*, 197–198.

18. Ibid., 201–202.

prophecy because the guidelines applied not only to what had happened but to what might happen. If one or more buildings in a particular area were in bad condition, it was assumed they would only get worse, so investment in that neighborhood was discouraged, both for new buildings and for repair. As a result it became difficult to sell property, and then values fell. If a building in an area colored red or yellow stood empty or fell into disrepair, this would seem to confirm the belief that property values invariably declined with any ethnic, racial, or income mixing.

In effect, the FHA discriminated against working-class and poor people in general, regardless of racial or ethnic background, and the agency unwittingly worked against many of the better-off people who owned property in Newark as well. Meanwhile, Newark suburbs were highly favored by FHA policies.[19] Cities across the country suffered in similar fashion.

Although Newark's population peaked in the 1930 census, when it was home to 442,000 people, within the next decade it lost 13,000 mostly upper-middle-class and middle-class residents, my family among them. The city has never recovered either the numbers or the affluence of those who left. The tax burden fell on fewer citizens, so rates increased, and naturally the result—poorer services and higher taxes—made life in the city less attractive and more people left. This cycle had begun before World War I, slowed during World War II, and dramatically increased at the war's end, thanks to government subsidies of middle-income housing outside the city. It was now cheaper to buy in the suburbs than to rent in the city, and tax laws allowed homeowners to deduct the interest on their mortgage payments from their taxable income. Since there was no deduction for renters, they were, and still are, in effect penalized for not owning, and people with the more expensive properties and larger mortgages receive the biggest tax breaks.

About 21,000 white residents of Newark moved to the suburbs between 1940 and 1950, when roughly 30,000 southern blacks moved into the city. During the next decade, about 33,000 whites

19. Ibid., 211.

left and roughly 62,000 more blacks came in. In the early 1960s a prominent housing expert noted that the dramatic increases in the number of black inhabitants in the cities "spark fears that they will overtake the whites everywhere, invade suburbia as well, attack its social status, and challenge the financial soundness of its real estate."[20] Though blacks still made up only 11 percent of the entire population, this fear helped keep the suburbs virtually closed to African Americans until the 1970s. And to this day low-income people, whatever their race, are zoned out of many privileged communities by development standards that make these areas too expensive even for middle-income people, such as the children who grew up there.

15 ▶ ▶ ▶

It is easy to get the impression that the descendants of Europeans have avoided the problems so widely associated with African Americans, especially because the black ghetto draws so much public attention. But whites account for a substantial percentage of the poor—70 percent in New Jersey. Some European immigrants and their descendants never did manage to climb out of poverty, and some who did or who inherited money were not able to hold on to it. Many blacks, in contrast, with skill, determination, and luck were able to better their families' situations: Carol's grandfather, for instance, managed to buy a city property on South Orange Avenue with money saved from his job down south and at the VA hospital. There he opened his Sweet Shop and settled the family in an apartment overhead.

For the majority of blacks living in Newark, however, the quality of life decreased from 1930 on, especially in the Central Ward. You can read virtually interchangeable comments about Newark's housing conditions in reports written twenty years apart. In some cases they are talking about the same buildings. The 1940 census found that almost a third of the housing units needed major repairs.[21] And in 1944 a report found that half of all black persons lived in "unhealthful and unwholesome quarters." Many had no private toilets or bathtubs, central heating was rare, and yet their owners collected high rents.[22] These were the same conditions my grandparents had lived with in

20. Abrams, *The City*, 56.
21. Groh, *Profiles of a Ghetto*, 166.
22. Cunningham, *Newark*, 299.

1923, though their rent was low. A later report found 1960 a better year to be poor than 1940, with better jobs and education and higher income, but housing was considerably worse. In the Central Ward, 91 percent of the buildings needed major repairs.[23] Eighty percent of the buildings had been built before 1929.[24]

After World War II, as Newark became blacker and poorer, the federal government became increasingly concerned about the decline of the cities and stepped up efforts to save them. The basic idea, which was developed in the 1930s, was to clear slums and build decent housing at rents the poor could afford. As good as this idea sounded to many people, it contained a fatal flaw: It did not provide a way to house people while they were waiting for construction to replace what had been torn down. As happened later on, superhighways ripped through the city, whole neighborhoods were razed, and the city lost more property tax revenues.

Other problems plagued the urban renewal program. For instance, collecting poor people into isolated groups made them more visible and even more dramatically associated with rundown neighborhoods than they had been, thus increasing the stigma of poverty.

In Newark, more units of public housing were built than in any other American city, and the Housing Authority won high praise in the 1940s and 1950s. For reasons that are unclear, however, routine maintenance was not performed, although nearly $100 million had been appropriated for that purpose. Now the majority of the buildings that have not been demolished stand half empty, monuments to incompetence and corruption, and are slated for demolition.

By the mid-1960s, it was obvious to many poor people that, despite good intentions, government programs to help poor neighborhoods were not working well, and they increasingly perceived themselves quite correctly as being victimized rather than helped. At the same time, my suburban neighbors were equally correct in seeing that millions of their hard-earned tax dollars were going up the chimney as problems in the inner city grew worse.

23. Groh, *Profiles of a Ghetto,* 166.

24. The Governor's Select Commission on Civil Disorder, *Report for Action* (Trenton: State of New Jersey, February 1968), 2.

In 1967 African Americans were still shut out from deciding who would manage their city and join its payroll. Widespread stories of corruption in city hall were confirmed during the trial of the mayor in 1970. Blacks were largely excluded from city jobs and construction crews. Poor health continued to be a serious problem; a major employer in the Newark metropolitan area blamed health problems for a third to a fourth of all rejections of job applicants, and a Welfare Department study attributed a third of the city's caseload to health factors.

In addition to these general and long-standing problems, two events generated widespread anger. An unqualified white politician was favored over a well-qualified black professional for the key job in the Newark school system,[25] and the proposal to demolish old buildings housing about five thousand people to make way for the New Jersey College of Medicine galvanized the black community.[26] Supporters of slum clearance spoke in glowing terms of their plans, and it must have been difficult for policymakers to imagine people wanting to hang on to this dilapidated housing. After all, it was the same area that my grandmother had left without a backward glance in the early 1920s. But the people living there worried about what would become of them, for they had already experienced what was cynically known as "Negro removal." Between 1960 and 1967, the number of vacant housing units had almost doubled in the core area of the city. Residents felt that even dilapidated shelter was better than nothing, and all too often nothing was what poor people got when government construction projects were underfunded and not completed. This complex situation provided the tinder for the riot of 1967.

The riot began in a city that had just celebrated its Tri-Centennial anniversary, and was sparked by a single incident on July 12, 1967. A black taxi driver was arrested for a driving violation and was badly beaten. Word of the beating spread, and anger against the police spilled over to shops, especially the ones owned by people whom ghetto dwellers felt were cheating them. Central Ward residents began

25. Ibid., 59.
26. Cunningham, *Newark,* 316.

rioting on the main shopping street, Springfield Avenue, where I and the people I know used to shop for wedding dresses, furniture, and appliances.

The governor of New Jersey responded to the emergency by sending in 5,367 National Guardsmen and 600 state troopers.[27] Reacting to reports of a single sniping incident, they sealed off fourteen square miles and, in the words of Police Director Dominick A. Spina, began "seeing snipers everywhere"—and shooting.[28]

From her apartment window, Carol, who was six years old at the time, spotted army trucks rolling down the streets and told her mother about them. At first her mother laughed at her, but seeing them from the window, she screamed and ran down the street to get Carol's fourteen-year-old brother, who had just gone to the store.

"The soldiers told my mother to get back upstairs," Carol recalls. "She came back . . . hollering and told us all to get under her bed." Carol remembers her brother returning loaded up with candy, Kool-Aid, and water guns. Later, soldiers came into the apartment looking for pilfered goods.

"I can still hear those army men hollering, 'Get away from those windows!'" says Carol.

> I was so scared under that bed. I still have dreams about that. The dream is always army trucks coming through here and rounding up the little kids, taking all the kids . . . and the soldiers are talking a foreign language. All the big trucks are full. They have kids in chains and the women are crying for their kids and the soldiers are killing their husbands. I can see everything so clear in this dream. I am hiding under the stairwell with my kids. Kason is little and I have my hand over his mouth and keep saying, "Don't cry, don't cry," while I hear the soldiers checking the houses. "Don't cry, don't cry." Then Kason bites my hand and I holler just as the guy is coming in the hallway. That's when I always wake up sweating and crying and crying.

27. The Governor's Select Commission on Civil Disorder, *Report for Action*, 118.
28. Ibid., 136.

When the riot ended, five days after it began, twenty-six people were dead—one white policeman, one white fireman, and twenty-four black civilians. Ten million dollars' worth of property damage left the Central Ward looking like a war zone.[29] Police Director Spina told the Governor's Commission that investigated the riots that the guardsmen "were firing at noises and firing indiscriminately at times."[30]

Tragically, the riot seemed to confirm the worst fears of both sides. For parents and children looking down the wrong end of rifles in the ghetto, it seemed that the government not only did not care about them but was actually out to destroy them. The ghetto residents called the riot a rebellion. To suburbanites, it confirmed beliefs about blacks being irresponsible, even dangerous. And many who once looked forward to seeing movies or eating out in Newark stopped going there, altogether, after dark.

Between 1970 and 1975, Newark suffered an additional loss of forty-two thousand residents, among them middle-class blacks. Once civil rights legislation opened some of the suburbs to African Americans, those who could take advantage of the opportunity for safer neighborhoods and better schools did so, generally pushing into nearby suburbs like East Orange and Irvington.

For Carol's grandmother also, the riot signaled the end. She had never liked Newark. She found it too closed in and "too rough." So she and her husband packed up their three unmarried daughters and left. With urban renewal money received for their Sweet Shop and a VA mortgage, they bought a small house in Piscataway, a town with a tiny black community and a good school system. Their daughters benefited from the move and are now settled in their own homes.

Carol's mother, Joyce, who married very young and never finished school, chose to stay in the city. She loved Newark and did not want to have anything to do with "the sticks." But the family paid a price for staying behind. Their lives were far more difficult than those of their suburban relatives.

Carol remembers moving from abandoned building to aban-

29. Ibid., 125.
30. Ibid., 136.

doned building as a child. Her father was a contractor and, says Carol, they always had a house.

> My father would walk around the neighborhood and find him a house that was boarded up, take down the boards, work on it for three months and move us in there, and not pay a dime for it. When somebody found out and told him he got to leave he'd find another one. Most of the time he tried to keep the houses he picked in the same school district, so we didn't have to change schools. So from kindergarten to the sixth or seventh grade I stayed in the same school.

For a few years during her teens, Carol stayed with her grandmother in Piscataway and during that time, she says, she got a good education.

Amazingly, parts of Newark have risen again in recent years, despite terrible odds. Black and white leadership helped save the city. Every weekday its gleaming towers draw many thousands of suburbanites in to staff white-collar jobs, and new buildings evoke pride. Unfortunately, an old problem still constricts Newark's recovery: the exemption of a large number of valuable properties from taxes. In 1991, about 76 percent of Newark property was tax exempt, an increase of 11 percent from 1978.[31] Colleges, universities, museums, libraries, parks, hospitals, churches, and government properties pay no taxes. And yet they require municipal services, which the city has to pay for. For example, the proposed tax-free site of the new $300 million cultural arts center in the downtown area will cost the city over $14.6 million in assessed property tax losses and call for an increase in city services.[32]

In the 1960s and 1970s, interstate highways 78 and 280 made it easier for suburbanites to go back and forth to work and attend colleges and other institutions, but they pay property taxes only in the suburbs. Knowing the downtown building activity would eventually increase tax receipts, Newark enticed companies into the city

31. Cunningham, *Newark,* 344.

32. Ibid., 368–370.

by giving them "attractive tax breaks,"[33] which worsened Newark's budgetary problem.

Newark hopes to offset some of the tax loss through a new, private University Heights development, forty-five acres of housing that will cost between $58,000 and $98,000.[34] As important as this project is, it still will not reach the very poor. The only major organization reaching this group is the New Community Corporation (NCC), founded after the riot by a dedicated group of Central Ward people, and led by a priest, William Linder, who decided to take a stand and rebuild the ward. The NCC is now a multifaceted organization with an annual budget of more than $100 million whose efforts, including modernized low-income housing, medical care, day-care services, job training, and a supermarket, are visible throughout the Central Ward. The NCC provides a rare and precious hope for people like Carol and her mother. Especially at a time when the traditional opportunities of getting up and out of the ghetto no longer exist—the jobs that paid a livable wage for unskilled, uneducated labor are gone.

Carol's mother has lived in the NCC's subsidized senior complexes for the past ten years, across the street from where Carol's grandfather's Sweet Shop once stood. Joyce loves living in a quiet, clean, safe building in her old neighborhood, a place that holds fond memories despite the hardships she faced growing up.

33. Ibid., 357.
34. Ibid., 371–372.

*Playing dress-up on Eagle
Street, September 1980*

▼
▼
▼

Photographs
► ► ►

► ► ►
Rebecca, January 1984

►►►

Arnetha, five years old,
November 1985

►►►

Rasheek painting apart-
ment, October 1985

Rasheek and Baby Kason,
May 1985

▼
▼
▼

▶ ▶ ▶

Arthur ("Diamond"),
November 1985 (froze to
death October 1987)

◀ ◀ ◀
Nicy and Elsie temporarily
living in an abandoned
bus, April 1986

▲
▲
▲

Rasheek reading to his
father, Keonda, and
Keisha, June 1986

► ► ►
Angie and her daughter,
April 1987

Joe holding child, May

1987

▼
▼
▼

Belinda and friends on

Johnson Avenue stoop,

June 1987

▼
▼
▼

▲
▲ ▲
▲

Ripple Field,
September 1987

*"Ring-a-round" in defunct
shower rooms, Ripple
Field, September 1987*

▼
▼
▼

▲
▲
▲

*Hermineo taking clothes
home to his mother in
their cardboard shack,
October 1987*

▲
▲ ▲
▲

*Carol's vestibule, May
1988. Left: unidentified
child, Carol, Sammy, and
Debbie fixing her son's
jacket*

*"We have no leader," May
1988. Top, left: Buck,
Jim, Sneed, Nathaniel
(killed January 1993).
Bottom, left: Clinton,
Roger, Duby (died April
1993), unidentified, and
unidentified*

▼
▼
▼

Flipping in Carol's back-
yard, May 1988

▼
▼
▼

▲
▲
▲

Kason washing dishes,
September 1988

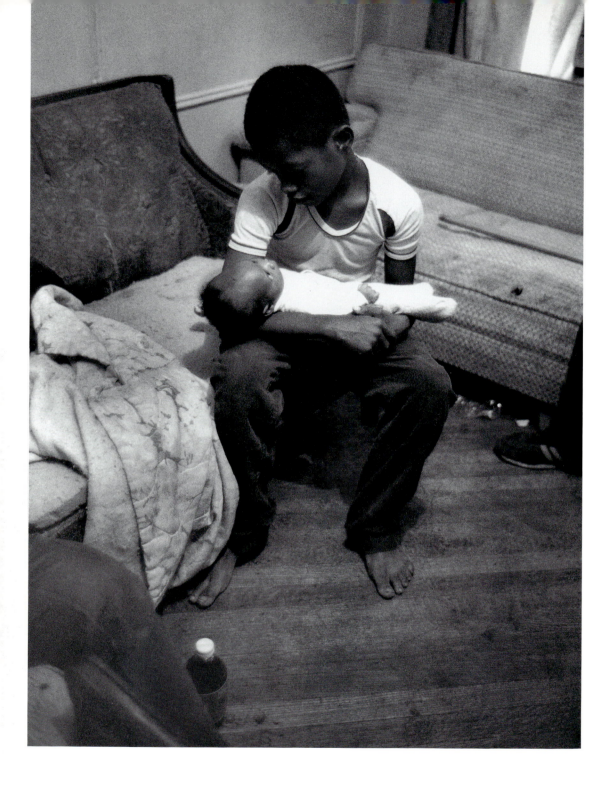

Noel and his sister,
Sharell, October 1988
◄ ◄ ◄

Stairwell in Rasheek's
parents' apartment build-
ing, Clinton Avenue,
November 1988

► ► ►

▲
▲
▲

Rasheek taking Kason to
preschool, December 1988

► ► ►
Kason doing his home-
work on a paper bag,
November 1989

"We want to be doctors."
Kason and Rashawn in
empty apartment across
the hall from Carol's place,
November 1989
▶ ▶ ▶

Homeless Mary,
November 1989
▼
▼
▼

▲
▲
▲
▲

Salvaging after a fire
on Hillside Avenue,
November 1989

▶ ▶ ▶

Carol helping Keisha,
Keonda, and Kason with
their homework,
December 1989

"I want to join the army."

Noel, December 1989

◄ ◄ ◄

▲
▲ ▲
▲

Glen, December 1989

Rasheek and Kason,

April 1990

▼
▼
▼

Carol looking out at
Veronica after she was
evicted, June 1990

Doris and Tino, Rasheek's
parents, June 1991

▼
▼
▼

▶ ▶ ▶

54 ▶ ▶ ▶

Omar, June 1991

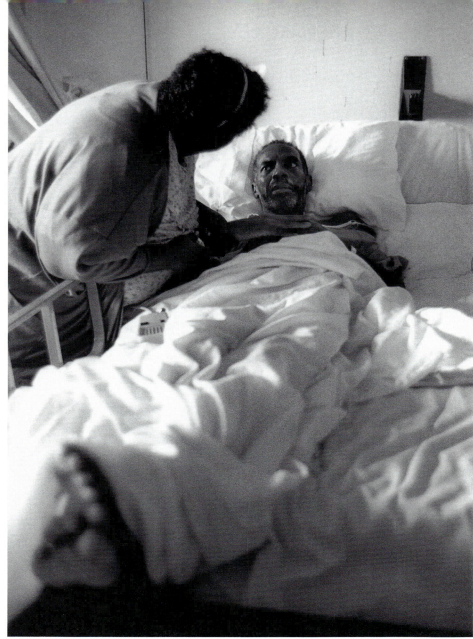

▲
▲
▲

"Don't worry, Daddy."
Carol visiting her father in
the hospital, June 1991

▶ ▶ ▶

Mary waiting for the
ambulance, June 1991

Carol putting prayer
note into grave wreath
for Rasheed's brother,
December 1991

▼
▼
▼

◄ ◄ ◄
Brittny, June 1991

▲
▲
▲

Robyn, Robert, and Latee-
fah playing in Carol's
backyard, October 1992

*"I'm grown now. I want to
be a model or a doctor."
Arnetha, twelve years old,
October 1992*

▼
▼
▼

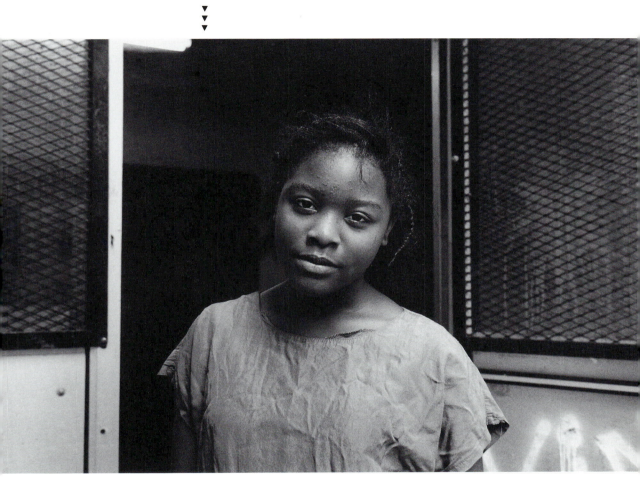

Christmas. Brittny and
Carol, December 1992

▲
▲ ▲
▲

"Don't run away from
your aunt again without
telling me." Carol and
Margo, January 1993

▲
▲ ▶ ▶
▲

Noel and Gina after a
fight, January 1993

▶ ▶ ▶

Carol studying for her
high school diploma,
March 1993

Carol's engagement to
Rasheek, March 1993

▼
▼
▼

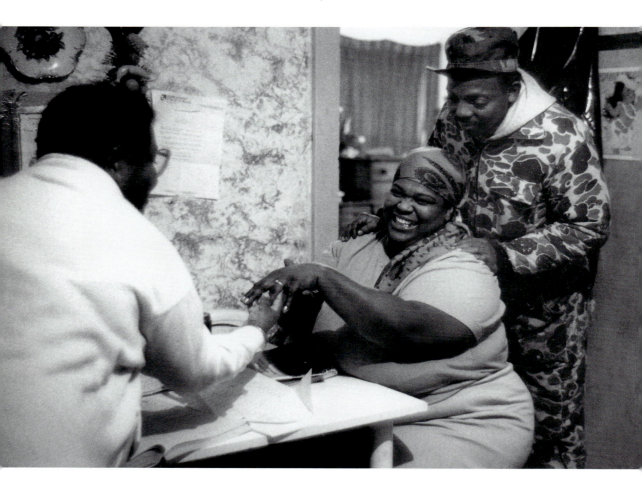

▲
▲
▲▶
▲

Easter Sunday, April
1993. Left: Shirka,
Keisha, Mary with baby,
Carol, and Keonda

Noel and Gina, May 1993

▼
▼
▼

►►►

Carol's altar,
October 1993

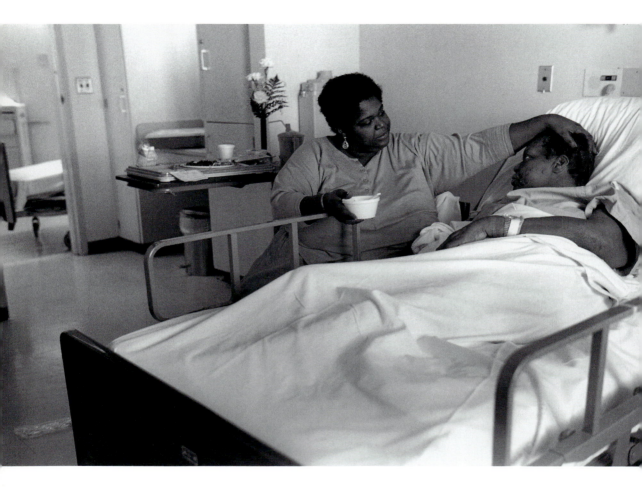

▲
▲
▲

Carol visiting her mother,

Joyce, in the hospital,

October 1993

*Tanya said, "A young
girl was just killed down
the street and nobody
knows who did it." Tanya,
Arnetha's mother, and
Arnetha's cousin Jermont
in "Hoodlum City" (Stella
Wright projects),
December 1993*

▼
▼
▼

Chapter 1
Carol's world

▶ ▶ ▶

The Central Ward of Newark, where Carol lives, is a short distance from the gleaming towers of the downtown renaissance and the well-maintained houses and lawns of suburbia. It looks like a different planet. Turning down the highway ramp each week on my way to Irvine Turner Boulevard, I plunge into a zone of empty lots, past hollow factories and abandoned houses. Children and adults wander among the ruins, some with the dazed expressions of war survivors. After ten years of coming here, I still feel the impact of this place as strongly as I did the first day I saw it.

Carol's street actually looked somewhat better when I first began photographing this block in 1983. Apartment houses stood on one side of her building, behind it, and across the street. Since then, most of these structures have burned down, one by one.

One other couple besides Carol and her family are the only people from those days still living in this twenty-four-unit building. Some have died; many families have broken up or have moved on; some have become homeless. The odds against a family holding on, surviving intact as a family, are almost overwhelming.

The cycle of abandonment and destruction is commonplace in the Central Ward. Frequently, a landlord will stop paying taxes and abandon a building for one reason or another. When this happens, people in the neighborhood "raze" it, taking anything that can be turned into money—wiring, plumbing, gutters. Many of these buildings are earmarked by the city for demolition, but they are left standing for years.

People in the neighborhood fear the abandoned buildings because they are fire traps that jeopardize the surrounding tenements. They also provide potential havens for drug pushers and child molesters. At the same time, however, these shells have some social value as a haven for homeless people, some of whom are relatives and friends of people living in the area. To people without homes, some shelter, no matter how miserable, is better than none.

Whenever there is a fire, rumors fly. After the last one, which was officially termed "suspicious," it was said that a suburban landlord had hired someone to "torch the place." Others thought that drug addicts living in the building had accidentally started the blaze while preparing their crack. Whatever the truth, fire remains a constant worry.

As more buildings burn down, the residents become increasingly concerned about being displaced by suburban developers. In 1988 they anxiously watched tractors and bulldozers piling up huge mounds of earth to begin construction of a shopping mall. "We need housing, not a shopping center," said one resident. "I can't believe it," said another person who lives nearby. "For sure, our children don't need to see firsthand what they can't have." They couldn't believe that the mall was intended for them, though it turned out that it was. The mall supermarket opened in 1989 and folded in 1991.

Just as suburbanites fear that poor people, whatever their color, will encroach on their neighborhoods, Carol and many of her neighbors now worry that wealthy suburban investors will take over their area and push them out. The beginnings of townhouse construction and groundbreaking for a six-movie complex convince them that the area can be fixed up for people with money.

"It's too bad we can't afford to live here when it's done," Carol says. Anticipating that later on her children won't understand why they had to move away from such a nice area, she is saving my pictures to show them when they grow up what this place was like when they were small. "Someday they're gonna ask me why we moved," she explains, "and I'm gonna show them the pictures of how it looked when we lived here."

"This area looks real bad," says one resident. "The suburbia folks drive this way every day from the highway to get to work downtown. When enough of these 'suspicious fires' have taken place, then the city will level the rest, widen the road, and build townhouses for the middle class. The mall will already be there for them. And what will they say? 'It's about time this place was cleaned up. Those people don't take care of nothin'—they got no pride.'"

Carol and her family

Not only her family but also many friends and neighbors depend on Carol to help them get messages to one another and to do other small favors. Beyond that, they turn to her when food runs out, when an eviction notice comes, or when they need an

Carol's world

74 ▶ ▶ ▶

ambulance. Crisis in this building is part of everyday life. And Carol is an expert in handling crises.

Born in Washington State in 1961, Carol spent most of her early years in Newark and came to this apartment building in 1981 with her baby daughter, Keisha. Pregnant with her second daughter, Keonda, she had left her husband because he was abusing her.

"I moved here," Carol recalls, "because this was the only place I could afford, after looking for three months." Her rent was $160 for two rooms and a kitchen. She received $283 from Aid to Families with Dependent Children (AFDC) for herself and her child, and $103 in food stamps. Fortunately, the landlord allowed her to pay off the security in $30 installments. It was over a year before she could save up $115 to have the lights turned on. "I stayed with my mother the first six months because I had no furniture or lights and I wasn't sleepin' on that stuff."

The furnished apartment had one dirty dresser in it and a dirty mattress, and it smelled of dead rats. But Carol remembers being so happy just to have a place of her own that she felt confident that a little paint and some soap and water would make the place look better. "It never really looked good," she said, "but at least it was clean." When Keonda was born a few months later, her AFDC allotment was raised by $60, bringing it to $343.

A couple of years later, Carol met Rasheek. "He just walked in one day telling me he liked the smell of the chicken I was frying," she recalls. "But I already had my eye on him. Of all the men that were standing around out there, he looked like he was about something. Like he wasn't going to be a wino all his life. I knew he had a job working as a ground man on the garbage truck. We knew he was making money. We wasn't stupid. I guess you could say it was an instant attraction." They began keeping company, and considering themselves engaged, they had a son, Kason, then Jonathan, who died at six weeks.

Rasheek was born in Newark and is the only person in his family to have finished high school. He has several children from relationships with other women but is in close contact only with his son Kareem.

Carol's and Rasheek's parents all live in Newark. A few years ago, their mothers, Joyce and Doris, sat next to each other at a family affair. They began comparing dates and places and, getting a good look at each other, realized that they had been best friends in grammar school. They still get along and see each other as often as possible.

Carol's rent (in 1991) is $475. Although the landlord says the 6 percent yearly increase is for maintenance, each month only one thing seems to get fixed just before the rent is collected. A two-bedroom apartment in the same building costs $525–$550 a month. The heat and hot water are unreliable, and the place is in chronic disrepair. The Health Violations Bureau has regularly cited the building for multiple violations, but often it is cheaper for the owner to pay the fine than to make the repairs.

Three years ago, Carol gave up drinking, after Baby Jonathan died. In an effort to improve her living situation, she spent two years trying to get her general equivalency diploma (G.E.D.) so she could become a nurse's aide. Initially, there was a problem with teachers not showing up. Carol became discouraged when, she said, a substitute gave the class the same test five times. "A test to see if we were eligible to take this course." But recently Carol transferred to another school and is doing very well working toward getting her regular high school diploma, which presumably enables people to earn a better wage than a G.E.D. does. Now she looks forward to her four school nights, getting dinner ready for her family, making arrangements for a babysitter, and finding transportation. She feels that she's "getting somewhere." In August 1991 Rasheek got his driver's license, and I gave him my old car. His hope is to work full-time for the city's sanitation department. Before, when he worked as a ground person, he just hung around until a driver needed help, and if he was chosen, he worked only that day. It's been four months since he filled out the application. Meanwhile, he continues with day jobs whenever he can find them.

Carol's tiny apartment is the first one in from the front entrance, a natural location for a clearinghouse, and her door is almost always open. She greets me with a shining smile, hugging me against her massive body. Today she's wearing a long black dress, her head is wrapped in a colorful scarf, and her red toenails shine on her bare feet. Though large, Carol moves in a light and graceful manner, her hands eloquently accentuating her stories.

It is not easy to have an extended conversation with Carol without being interrupted because there is often "standing room only." Neighbors, friends, relatives, and people who have moved away in the ten years she's been here continue to depend on her. Because having a telephone and getting one's mail are privileges rarely enjoyed in the ghetto, people leave messages with Carol: "Please tell Joe that job I told him about is available." "Please give this note to Nathaniel." "When she comes by, tell my daughter I'll pick her up tomorrow." Sometimes the requests are urgent. One day Mary burst in with: "Please call the ambulance for me, Carol. I'm losing my baby."

Carol does much more than help people keep in touch. On one particular day, in a matter of about fifteen minutes, I watched the following exchanges: first, Carol handed a cigarette down from her window to a woman on the sidewalk who had just been evicted and sent her son, Kason, down to fetch the woman's thermos and fill it with water. Then another woman came in crying that "her love" had taken her car and "he ain't never coming back."

"I know you love him," Carol said, "but you just started a new job, and you have got to keep yourself together."

"Yes," the woman replied, "that's why he's mad at me, since I got a job and make more money than he does."

"That sounds like a baby to me," Carol continued, putting her arm around the woman. "Do it on your own, forget him—you're strong."

"Yes," she responded, smiling through her tears. "Yes I am. Bless you, Carol."

After she left, Carol observed, "I have to close the door and the windows and let them knock because I got to take time for myself—get myself together." I couldn't help thinking how different it is where I live, how it would be normal for two weeks to go by without a knock on my door.

Next, a child appeared in the doorway with a cup in his hand. "My momma needs stuff to clean her clothes, please." Just as Carol was pouring some detergent into the cup, another child came in. "My momma sent a note—we have nothin' to eat."

Carol gave her some food, and when the child left she said, "I know that some of the parents spend their money on drink or dope, but what am I supposed to do when a hungry child is standing in front of me?" Sometimes in situations where parents sell food for dope, Carol cooks the food first and sends small amounts to the family, or she feeds the children in her kitchen.

A stream of other neighbors came by, one for a pencil, another for a piece of paper, another to put something in Carol's freezer, and yet another to ask her if she would go to church with her that night.

Another time, Rasheed, a thirty-year-old neighbor, came to Carol's door holding a grave wreath. He asked if Carol wanted to include her name in the wreath. I could see other pieces of paper sticking out of it. Carol wrote her name and blessings on a white piece of paper, pinned it to a couple of artificial flowers, and inserted it in the wreath (photo, p. 59). The man had tears running down his face, and Carol asked him if he was sure he could go through with visiting the grave today. He nodded yes. "Well I'll be here when you get back in case you'll need to talk," said Carol.

After Rasheed left, Carol told me that this was the fourth anniversary of his brother's death, and it was the first time that he felt able to handle the emotion of going to the grave. He was Rasheed's only brother, and they were very close. Rasheed was in jail when his brother committed suicide four years ago, and his mother was afraid to tell him in case they wouldn't let him out of jail to go to his brother's funeral—she was afraid he would "flip out." Rasheed has not spoken to his mother since. "In many ways, she lost two sons," said Carol.

I don't take Carol's generous nature for granted. Two years ago, I recall her screaming at her children. It was at the end of the Christmas holiday, and, unhappy with my negatives from the previous week, I asked Carol if she would mind sitting by the tree and letting me take more pictures, even though I had seen her three times that past week and taken more shots than usual. Each negative came closer and closer to exactly what I had in my mind, and I wanted that one "just right" shot. My intuition told me I was pushing it. "I'm not moving." Her words squeezed through her teeth. "You must have enough by now!" And she let fly a string of curse words relating to her children's behavior that I think was also meant for me. I murmured an apology, said good-bye, and crept out of her apartment.

So far, Carol continues to hold things together, but I wonder sometimes how much responsibility she can take. Her parents have been separated for many years. Her mother, though lucky to be living in a senior citizen complex, had her leg amputated because of complications from diabetes. Her father has spent the past three months in the hospital recovering from multiple stab wounds inflicted during a robbery attempt in his apartment. Rasheek's parents' building has just been abandoned by the landlord, and they are pressing to find another place to live.

Carol doesn't mind living in Newark. "I live near my mother," she said. "And there are a lot of people here who need my help. But I wish I could find a bigger place, one that was fixed up, one that was safe."

People in the ghetto are all older than their years. Sitting in Carol's kitchen one day, I listened to Carol and some neighbors talk about aging. "I'm thirty and I'm old," said Carol. "The everyday strain ages us all. Look at the children. Even the children are old."

Growing old

"I'm eighteen," said Mary, a mother of two children who had just had her third miscarriage, "and I feel real old."

"So do I," said another, who was thirty-four.

"Fifty in the outside world is not old," one commented, "but fifty down here is real old."

For many old people in the ghetto, sitting and drinking on the sidewalk with friends is about the extent of their day. They don't have money to go anywhere. With anything they can collect among themselves, they get a little bottle and sit outside on milk crates under one of the few trees left in this area and end up getting drunk. Then they get loud, and the teenagers tease them. "When they're drunk and staggering, that is funny for the kids," said Carol, "and they get to laughing. Then the old folks get pissed off. 'Hey! I'm old enough to be your grandfather.'"

Watching the old people outside Carol's window one day, I wondered aloud what it must be like to be dependent on public assistance, to have to spend years of your life wandering through the maze of bureaucratic offices, constantly filling out forms, constantly answering questions, and always being at the mercy of bureaucrats' decisions. They determine whether you will receive housing, health care, welfare, food stamps, social security, disability, or help in the legal departments. "They go by their own standards," Carol said.

> They don't have a humanity feelin' in there—they only know how to go by the book. But in reality poor people can't live by their books. When those people are confronted with reality they put up their guard and put that book in front of them and say, "That's it—I can't do no more than what this book say, I'm sorry." And you're caught out there. But most don't want to see the desperation. They never take their guard down and look at what is in front of them. If they did, they would take those rule books and put them in the back room somewhere and see what they can do for these people. When they do this, something will happen.

This conversation reminded me of the one time I had to collect unemployment benefits. I remember how I worried about the time on my parking meter. Would it run out before I got to the head of the line? If it did, would the people around me hold my place? Did I have enough money for it? In the meantime, the whole line could hear the man who was processing checks making loud, hostile remarks. With each new applicant he became more brazen: "Are you sure you wasn't sitting around all day? I wish *I* could just pick up a check for doing nothing! Are you sure you really want to work?"

As the hours dragged by, parents became less and less successful in distracting their tired and fretful children. On and on the rude remarks went, the man's grating voice vibrating throughout my nervous system. I became angry as I thought about the multitude of problems and injustices that had brought me there in the first place. I wanted to tell him what I thought of his offensive behavior, but I was afraid that it would jeopardize my check. So, like everyone else, I kept quiet.

As I turned away from Carol's window, even though it was a bright sunny day, the apartment looked dark. One bare bulb hung down from the high ceiling. I always have to sit at the opposite end of the kitchen table so my shadow doesn't eclipse the dim light. Often I use my tape recorder because I can barely see the paper I am writing on.

While I sat at Carol's kitchen table, the usual steady stream of people came and went. I asked Carol if she could tell me more about what it's like for her parents now that they are both ill.

"Almost every day I've been taking my mother to visit my father in the hospital," she reported. Her mother has been more or less helpless since her leg amputation two years ago. She is fifty-two.

"I see a lot of sufferin' when I see them together," Carol reflected.

It just make me sad they can't do nothin' for themselves. She's in a wheelchair and he's paralyzed on the left side. They just lookin' at each other. She's trying to feed him water. She can't just get up and go over there and do it. She's hanging all out of the wheelchair trying to hold the straw and making sure she ain't slip out of the wheelchair. And he's there tryin' to get the water but he can hardly move. It's a hurtin' feeling.

Carol's mother gets mad at her if she doesn't take her to the hospital every day. "But it's hard for me," said Carol.

She weighs 300 pounds. Getting her in that car, putting in that king-size wheelchair—I got to pick that thing up and put it in

the back of my station wagon, take her over to the hospital, park
the car, take her out, lift it out, put it in front of the car, put her
back in it, and I got to do the same thing coming back. I'm so
tired. My back is hurtin'. My legs are hurtin'. It takes me four
hours. That's a whole afternoon. I got three small children to
raise. I ain't got the time.

Many of the women in the room said that their parents also
had become dependent on others, that they just couldn't take care of
themselves. They needed help with the basics—shopping, cleaning,
and cooking. Some of their parents also had had strokes and seizures.

Carol's father never depended on anybody for anything. "Now,"
she said,

he needs a shave, his hair is messy. He looks old. He's about
fifty-six. I never saw my father look like that. He never looked
old before. The age really show now. Then my sisters are talking
about putting him in a nursing home. I couldn't stand having
him go to a nursing home and have somebody else take care of
him. He's not disabled, where he be right under your way all
the time. He's got his own mind. He can think. He knows what's
right and wrong. He can hold his own cup. He can feed his own
self. In a nursing home they push you by a window and leave
you there. His momma wanted to take him back to Florida with
her, but she is eighty-nine and isn't right. She needs somebody
to take care of her.

When Carol's mother gets quiet, as she does from time to time,
Carol knows she's disgusted with her situation.

I never pity her, only when she's depressed. Then I baby her up
a little, buy her something, tell her everything's gonna be okay,
until I get so tired from doin' for her I get mad at her. And then
I tell her, "Listen, all you had was an amputation. The rest of
your body is workable. So won't you go and get your leg out?"
They gave her a leg. She don't like the leg because it's black and

she yellow skin. When she put it on she got one black leg and one yellow leg. The black leg is real big and *her* leg is real little. It's like two mismatched socks. So she ain't like it. She says it hurts when she put it on by her joint where she got cut off at. I say, "Why you ain't take that leg back and let them fix it? That leg cost the state over two thousand some dollars and you ain't using it."

Carol went on discussing her mother's situation.

There's a guy in her building who had an amputation on his leg the same year that she had hers, and about the same time. He got out of the wheelchair. She don't wanna get out of the bed. When she came home, she was in the bed.

"I ain't movin'," she says. "I ain't gonna have nobody laugh at me. I'm stayin' in my bed."

She was in her bed for three months when that man said to me, "Your mother ain't out of that bed yet? I'm comin' up there with you."

He told her, "You get up out of that bed now. You can't let that leg make you lay up in the bed like that. Mine don't. I just got home two months ago too and I ain't layin' down."

So he talked to her, talked to her, talked to her, and I flipped out. She was comin' out the bedroom in the wheelchair. I looked at that man. He's walking around even without a cane. He said, "I got places to go and people to see."

"See, Momma, how he do that?"

"I don't know," says my mother. "That leg get me down."

It's a hurtin' feeling. The other day in the hospital my father said, "I want to get out of this chair." He was tied to the chair. He said, "Loosen me up!"

"Daddy, the nurse said you can't get out of the chair or you might loosen that feedin' tube connected to your stomach."

"I want to get out of this chair," he hollered, "and get into bed. I've been sittin' here all day."

I came back from the nurse and told Daddy: "She said you can't get out of the chair."

My mother said, "Why he can't get out of the chair?" I'm lookin' at her. "Why you askin' me why he can't get out of the chair for?" "Oh lighten up child, he wants to get out of the chair." If I let him up, I'm gonna get in trouble. I look at my mother. "Just loosen your daddy, okay?" Then Daddy says, "If your brother was here I'd already be in that bed." Now I'm really feeling bad. So I loosen him. I took the whole thing right off of him. I think my mother got a plan for me. She's thinking he gonna stay with her, and I can come over and take care of everything. Every day.

The next day I saw Carol again. I was following through with my observation that every day brings a major problem in the ghetto.

"So how you doing today, Carol?"

"Oh, not so good. Rasheek's family needs to move out of their building. They want to move here. They said, 'Get me an apartment.' They expect him to find them a place. No, I can't deal with this.

"Rasheek said, 'They're old and they want to move in here.' I say, we must be movin' out then, 'cause I ain't staying here. Not me!" Pacing back and forth in the tiny kitchen, Carol continued.

I can't take them. His mother is the type that me and Rasheek can be arguing over something, which we do quite often because he do things he ain't suppose to do, and she tells me, leave her son alone. In my own house she tells me that! He goes to see them and he comes back being mad at everybody for a week. Can you imagine him with them living here? And every day they'd be down here for something to eat. I can't take that.

A few days later, Carol said she was going to visit her father and told me to come along if I wanted to take some pictures. On our way to the hospital, driving along Bergen Street, I was devastated to see row after row of new garden-type apartments boarded up. Especially when there are so many people in desperate need of shelter. I asked Carol what was going on. "The plumbing was put in wrong," she said, "and now nobody can live in them." Somebody else told me that they were priced too high—you had to have a yearly income of nineteen thousand dollars. And the rooms were tiny; you could barely fit a double bed in the bedroom. Still another person mentioned that these apartments were built by a nonprofit community program with HUD (the federal Department of Housing and Urban Development) codes, and they're not getting any buyers because they're priced too high. She wondered why they can't just rent them out. According to Harold Lucas, director of the Department of Development, they "anticipate total project sellout by summer 1992."

When we reached the hospital lobby, we scrounged to come up with five dollars for flowers from an automatic dispenser: two white carnations, some baby's breath, and a glass vase with water in it. Carol's father had been here for three months. I had never met him. I introduced myself and asked for permission to take his picture (p. 56). He nodded yes.

My first impression of Teddy was how good looking he was in spite of his condition, and how small he was. Carol and her mother are large people, and I just assumed that he would be the same. He was delighted to see Carol. He held on to her hand as though it were a life raft. He told her he was going back to Florida with his mother, that she was on her way up to get him.

"That's okay, Daddy," said Carol. "We'll visit you."

"I love you," he said quietly. "I'm going to miss you awful."

"It's okay, Daddy. We'll come for vacation."

Then he asked Carol to put water in the vase of dead roses. He hadn't noticed our gift. "Flowers should be alive," he said. "Please bring me some fresh flowers."

We moved the white carnations so he could see them, and he smiled. As we were getting ready to leave, Teddy held Carol's arm and cried and cried. "Please, Daddy, don't cry, the Lord is with you. Everything will be all right." After a while, they waved good-bye to each other and smiled. Two steps away from the door, Carol sobbed, "I never saw my father cry before. It hurts so bad."

Chapter 2
Home sweet home
▶ ▶ ▶

Ghetto hallways are terrifying places. As soon as I open the door to the foyer of Carol's building, my body tenses, my breathing becomes shallow. The door slams shut behind me and leaves me feeling trapped. Always there is that feeling of being cornered, confined, with no escape in the face of danger.

It is a relief to find people waiting in the foyer for the mail. Most of the mailboxes are broken, and the carrier has not put mail in them for years. Carol once explained to me what can happen if you don't wait in the foyer at delivery time.

> If the carrier calls out Mary Smith, and I say, "I'm Mary Smith," or I say, "I'll give it to her," he will give me her check. That happened to me twice. My check came back cashed without my signature on it. I don't know how they do that, but they do. So we're out there. Also, the carrier will give the mail to the super, and if he has a "bug on," if he's angry, he will throw it on the floor and we all have to scramble for it.

Unlike most days, Carol's door is closed, and I notice, for the first time in all these years, that there is no doorknob. "A doorknob is a big expense when you're worried about food on the table," she told me once. "The landlord says that he will reimburse us if we buy one, but he never will. Mostly he says if we don't like it here, just move."

Waiting for someone to answer my knock, I begin to feel uncomfortable again. The hall is dim and grimy with an antiseptic smell reminding me of custodial institutions. Unnerving images of the three upper floors come to mind; Carol and Rasheek holler at me if I go up there alone because it is so dangerous. On those floors, tenants often have to use cigarette lighters to find their locks. Apparently the drug dealers remove the light bulbs so they can mug and deal with ease. The sounds of yelling, screaming, crying, and doors slamming echo throughout the building.

Switching from pounding with my fist to tapping as loud as I can with my key, I begin to wonder, since nobody seems to be responding, who would hear me if I had to scream for help. The television and fan inside are hard to compete with. I knock even louder. The sound of footsteps on the stairs alerts me to the possibility of danger, but it's only nine-year-old Ernest. We greet each other, and I try to engage him in conversation, but he is in a hurry. Then, just as I feel at wits' end, the door opens. Carol tells me to knock louder next time as she welcomes me into safety.

Carol acknowledges my fear and tells me that when her friend Mary goes back to her fourth-floor apartment, she stays by her own door until Mary hollers down the stairs that she has her door open. Then Carol yells up that she is also okay, and they both slam their doors.

If people scream, Carol says, she doesn't do anything about it. Once, after she had been living in the building for about a year, she heard two men arguing loudly outside her door, and then one shot the other. She heard the killer run out the back and didn't open her door until the police came. They wondered why she hadn't heard anything, since there was blood all over her door. She lied and said she was watching television.

For parents, it is a constant struggle to teach children about the dangers of the hallways: "If you have to go to another apartment and there's a group of men standing around, don't go past them. Come back to your own place, and get a grown-up to go with you." "Don't run on the stairs, they're ready to cave in." "Don't slide on the bannisters, they're rotted and ready to fall apart." "Don't pick up any of those yellow or blue papers. There can still be some dope in them." The kids are fascinated by the wrappers. They like to see how many of each color they can find. Naturally, they want to touch them, and then they put their fingers in their mouths. Being on the first floor, Carol would rather have her children play on the sidewalk, where she can watch them, than in the hallway. "Out in the open nobody can pull them into an empty apartment," she explains. "We don't know everyone who lives here. The woman could be out and the man get lustful and pull a kid into his place."

I have been in many buildings where the tenants have to cover the broken windows with cardboard or plywood to keep the children from falling out. Fortunately, Carol's building has glass in most of the windows.

As dangerous as the hallways are, the foyer at least provides a place to gather, especially when it's raining outside. Although the tenants usually pass the time of day together, there is an atmosphere of mutual distrust. Everyone knows that one telephone call could start an investigation that could totally disrupt their lives. Sometimes a desire for revenge following a simple argument will motivate a person to call the welfare department and report that a man is living with "so-and-so." This could lead to suspension of their welfare checks pending an investigation. Or children could be taken away as a result of a call to the Division of Youth and Family Services (DYFS) complaining that so-and-so is hitting her child. Or someone could be arrested after a call telling the authorities that so-and-so has been seen selling drugs.

People are afraid of having their welfare checks stopped until an investigation is completed. Officially, this cannot happen until that person is notified, but it doesn't always work out that way. Carol says that once a check is stopped, people have a hard time getting payments reinstated. Reinstatement can take months.

Street life

The street is an extension of the dangerous hallways. Carol worries about the street's influence. She knows how one's environment and friends can affect what one decides to do. "Rasheek can get in trouble hanging around on the street," she said. "Friends start talking, 'let's do this,' or, 'let's do that.' You go along." Says Carol,

> I told kids not to write on the walls in the hallway. The next day one of them wrote his name all over my car windows with black magic markers. Or they will mess with your child when you send her to the store. It's better to keep your mouth shut. Adults

see the wrong but it's fear of what will happen that keeps them quiet. Then the children lose respect for their parents when they see them back down. Already my seven-year-old Kason is showing traits of a street kid. The attitude is in his walk, like, "Nobody can touch me." One day he bumped into me with that walk, saying something about being in his way. Grabbing him by the collar, I forgot he only seven. I told him, "You better say excuse me! You hear!" I keep my children in the house and other kids call them sissies. Every tough person I know is in the ground. It's bad to tell a black child to be a sissy. They're suppose to have pride. I tell mine to be a sissy. A sissy will live. A sissy will wear a white collar.

I walked to the grocery store with Keisha one afternoon, and on the way back we passed a group of teenagers hanging around the corner. Carol had told me earlier to look straight ahead when I passed the men at the end of the street. "They're into dope and it isn't safe," she said. One of the young men called to me, "Hey! don't you remember me? Take a picture." I turned and there was Jim. I had photographed him in 1988 with his friends—"We have no leader" (p. 39). Also, he was in some of the flipping pictures. I was excited to see him. After I photographed Jim with some of his friends, I asked where Clinton was. Jim yelled down the street. Clinton came riding toward us on a bike, and I photographed him. I asked about Nathaniel (who had been in the group when I took their picture). He was shot in the head and found dead in a ditch in Pennsylvania, where he had recently moved, they told me. Nobody knew the details. When I brought back the pictures of Clinton on the bike the following week and showed the group picture from when they were younger, I found out that Duby had been killed when the stolen car he was riding in crashed.

Funerals are common in the ghetto. Just recently, fourteen-year-old Noel lost four friends. Three burned to death when the stolen car they were riding in crashed. The other one was shot to death for no apparent reason. Noel has been talking to me for years about wanting to move away from this area (p. 50). Five years ago, when he was nine, he said, "I wish we wasn't livin' in the city—too much drug and diseases goin' round. Some people don't like each other—they kill. I saw people kill—a man got killed and a woman got stabbed in the back with a knife. I remember that."

One day, talking to Sam, I asked what had happened to the young man seated nearby in a wheelchair. "He's paralyzed. Last year while we were hanging out on this corner a car drove by and started shooting at us. We scattered. But Larry caught a bullet in his back."

Another day, while I was photographing a group of teenagers in front of Carol's building, I noticed a police car parked a block away with its lights flashing. Then a car went by us so fast that I was astounded that anyone could drive at that speed with all the traffic around, and the police car pulled out and sped past us just as fast. One of the teenagers yelled out that the "dude" in the stolen car was wearing a jacket just like his. He took off his jacket and threw it on the ground. "I don't want them coming back here and thinking I was in the car," he explained.

"Kids wouldn't steal cars if the police didn't chase them," he added. "That's the fun. We do what we're told not to do. It's like when my mother tells us we can't go out. We go out."

Several days later, while watching some children wrestle on a car hood, I was talking with another child about her future. A man walked by wielding a five-inch knife. The children said they were scared, but when I told the adults, they just shrugged. If that had happened in my neighborhood, the response would be blinding and deafening. In a matter of minutes a half dozen police cars would show up with sirens blaring and lights flashing.

In this neighborhood, people are often harassed by the police. Sometimes they tell the women to pull their bras away from their bodies and jump, supposedly to see if they are hiding any drugs. One August night, some women and children were sitting outside to escape the heat indoors. Police cars pulled up, lights flashing, and the women were told to "spread eagle." One of the women was holding her baby, and the officer said she shouldn't have the child outside where drug deals were taking place. He threatened to take the baby to DYFS, but suddenly the car just pulled away.

Molestation is a constant worry. "I have to call the police as soon as I get this pervert's license plate number," said Carol. "Every year when school opens up the perverts ride around here. This one with red hair parks by the crosswalk right on the corner, shaking his thing in the car. The children see that as they stand there waiting for the light to change. I want the police to come and pick him up."

I asked Carol about the smashed-up cars in the neighborhood and whether what I'd heard is true—that outsiders hire ghetto kids to steal cars. "Nobody has to hire the kids to steal cars around here," she replied. "The kids do it themselves. There are some areas where they do take cars to the chop shop and all that kind of stuff. But here, they steal cars just for the fun of it—ride them around in the empty lots and just tear them up."

If they're not getting any cash out of it, why do the children do it? "Because they have nothing else to do," one parent said. "There's no recreation. There is one boys' club down here. The big kids don't go in there because the boys' club kicks them out 'cause they can't handle them. They can't handle their attitude. Teenagers are wild 'cause the kids out here are ghetto kids. They got to get an organization that can deal with the teenage ghetto children problems. You can't take teenagers that are stealin' cars and doin' all this stupid stuff and put them in a little boys' club and tell them to play basketball."

Later, as I was sitting with a group of people in front of Carol's building, struggling to talk over the heavy traffic, ambulance and police sirens, and ice-cream truck music, several parents spoke about the problems they have with their children—how they don't listen. It seems that not listening to the counselors is what gets them kicked out of the boys' club.

Another parent spoke about how angry the children feel over being thrown out of the club. I mentioned how anger complicates the already difficult job of trying to teach discipline. How can a parent teach anything to a bitter and resentful child? The more trouble they get into, the more hardened children become. Vanessa nodded in agreement and murmured slowly, "And the only alternative is the streets."

"The streets are always open and waiting," Carol added.

"In this neighborhood," said another woman, "if you don't have someone to encourage you, you're lost, and when you're lost you get mean."

When they are incensed, children can become destructive, turning to common street activities here: vandalizing and selling drugs.

Ah! The drug problem. Everyone talked at once. "They got to give these welfare mothers enough money to take care of their kids," said Vanessa. The kids have trouble going to school because often they are hungry or have trouble staying awake. "But if they stay home, they can make fifty dollars selling a hundred of those little packs," Carol said. "Not only can they buy their momma dinner, but they can help with other family needs."

As the children ran up to the ice-cream truck, another woman mentioned the day when Brittny (p. 58) and other children were playing out front and drug dealers began shooting at the front of the building to remind someone inside that this was their territory. Carol's friend started screaming at the dealers to "kill each other if you want to, but let me get the children inside first." She said, "If the children were taller they would be dead."

As the stories continue amid this stark and broken neighborhood, I feel the heat of outrage well up in me. How can this place be so close to where I live and yet be light years away? I listen as Carol slowly and quietly relates the story about Margo being raped by two men when she was ten years old. She told her mother not to call the police because the men would come and kill them all. She also wouldn't go to the hospital, and later she tried a couple of times to commit suicide. "Since she was raped," Carol continued, "Margo seems to have lost her spirit. She's not like a normal teenager. There's something dead in her."

A new crisis comes when children reach eighteen. At that point, teenagers are automatically taken off welfare and become a total drain on their family. Many mothers are forced to tell their sons to get out of the house because they can't care for them anymore. So they're on their own. "I don't gotta put up with you anymore," I heard a mother shout. "Get out! You're eighteen. If you're bleedin', call me. Otherwise, leave me alone." As a parent, I can imagine the desperation of being in that situation. In order to survive, these parents have to go against their basic instinct and obligation to protect their children.

At fifteen, according to the mothers, the preparation for being kicked out begins. The attention shifts to the younger children, and the fifteen-year-old gets less to eat. At the end of the month, the teenager has to let the little kids eat first.

So what happens to the children who have reached the supposed age of maturity? They're in the street. Doing what? "Robbin', stealin', killin', anything 'cause they got to survive," said Carol. "It all boils down to survival from the age of fifteen on up. Ghetto is a survival game. You got to learn how to survive."

The females are just as affected by pressure to get out or pitch in, one woman told me. Unless a child has been able to rise above what is commonly seen in her environment, as occasionally happens with help, a fifteen-year-old girl, who is usually desperate for love and attention, says Carol, will get her pleasure from sexual activity. "She ends up pregnant the first time. Nobody told her it only take one time before it happens. Then she's pregnant, and out of school. It's a vicious cycle. She'll go on welfare and have the same problem with her own kids."

As the conversation continued around me, and the commuter traffic leaving Newark increased, I focused on the neighborhood. No one here knows the feeling of going out into the backyard and quietly relaxing, or even taking a walk, without plugging into their "survival record." This is the record that "plays in your head every time you get on the street," Carol explained. "You can never put your guard down. You can't keep your eyes down. You need to watch everything. Only the strong survive in the ghetto."

After yesterday, I am convinced that photographs do not represent this world the way it really is. They cannot possibly show the horror of living in an abandoned building.

I wanted to photograph Rasheek's parents, Doris and Tino, so Carol rode with me the few miles to their place. On the way, she told me that their building has been officially abandoned and that she has been looking for another apartment for them. They have lived in this place for the past five years. Even though Tino has a pension from working thirty-five years for the sanitation department, plus a small monthly disability check, they have a hard time making ends meet. Now the city has taken the building over for nonpayment of taxes, and the water, electricity, and heat will soon be cut off. The landlord came by recently to collect the rent—if they didn't give it to him, he said, he would take them to court. They were scared, so they gave him the $525, and now they don't have the money to put down on another apartment.

As we walked up to the building, I was stunned. I will never get used to seeing such devastation. I looked through my viewfinder, but this gave me only a limited sense of what I saw around me, an impression, and nothing about how it feels to be close to a rotting building. For one thing, what I saw through the viewfinder failed to show how open the structure was to the weather or to anyone who wanted to enter. Most of the steps going up to the hall were missing. The glass in the windows were gone. As we walked to their first-floor apartment, we passed a unit that was open and vacant. There was no door on the frame going out to the courtyard on my left, only piles of garbage. The place reeked of mildew and urine. I took a few quick pictures while Carol was knocking on their door. Instinctively I knew they were not good shots. I heard something heavy being dragged away from the door.

The limits of photography

95 ▶ ▶ ▶

Doris greeted us warmly. Walking in, I noticed a large dresser pushed slightly away from the door and realized what had caused the scraping sounds when we arrived. Of course. People in the ghetto often shove furniture in front of their doors for protection.

It was like walking into a cave; all I could see were indistinct shapes in the gloom. There seemed to be many people in the front room. We passed into the crowded bedroom, which held piles of belongings: a blaring television, the parents' double bed, and a sofa where others slept. Some kind of heavy material covered the two windows, and I noticed a paper American flag on the wall and a plant on the windowsill.

Aiming the camera to photograph Rasheek's parents, I tried to include the broken plaster on the walls and ceiling but couldn't get back far enough. I wanted to get in the broken screens as well, but there were only a couple of spots where it was possible to stand, and one was right in front of the window. Unfortunately, there was slow film in the camera, and even after I pulled the curtains back it was still very dark. The negatives later turned out to be unusable.

After finishing the first roll of film, I changed to one with a faster speed; feeling that I had intruded long enough, I took just one more picture in the bedroom. The parents looked fine in that shot, but just as I pressed the shutter a child climbed onto the sofa and spoiled the composition. As I got ready to leave, I noticed that the kitchen seemed a little brighter and asked Doris and Tino if they would allow me to take a few pictures of them in that room. Doris went to the stove and Tino sat down at a table close to where I was standing (p. 54). But how would I show the way the window material seemed to hold up the jumble of broken screens, glass, and wooden frames?

On my way out, thanking everyone and apologizing for my intrusion, I noticed a child who told me she was seven years old and that her name was Kewana. She looked at me in that heart-gripping way that I had seen before—trustful, innocent, tired. No one objected to my photographing her in the hall. Again I wrestled with my worry that I might be taking advantage of the family. But here I was, with this delicate child, surrounded by broken glass, debris, gray dirty walls—a shell of a building. Heaven and hell were here in front of me, and I became extremely anxious about failing to show it.

Walking among the ruins, Kewana looked at me in a way that made it clear that she wanted me to tell her what to do. So I asked her to stand by the window while I moved farther up the stairs, trying to frame her in my viewfinder. Voices drifted down. "What are you taking pictures for?" They repeated the question several times before I responded: "I'm doing a book about Newark." They grumbled something about the landlord and then all was quiet.

I continued in my confusion, my mind whirling. I wanted the child against the garbage, or against the torn open front door, any place that would really show her environment. She stood against the wall. The light wasn't very good, I came in close, she made a peace sign. I stopped photographing peace signs years ago, but I took this one. Then she stood under a *No Loitering* sign. Frustrated, I thanked her, gave her a handful of change, and Carol and I left.

On the way to the car, Carol yelled to the young guys on the corner, "I saw you grow up. Get off that corner! I'm sick of seeing our young black men on corners." They waved and smiled. When the traffic forced me to slow down, Carol called out, "Pray for me!" to a woman going into a church. "I sure will," she responded, waving.

Before going home, I stopped at Carol's apartment for a few minutes. Coming in, there is only a narrow space to walk between the beds and dressers in order to get to the kitchen. Carol's bedroom is off the kitchen. In the winter it is freezing, today it is suffocating. The front windows are closed, a fan is on. While she talked to Rasheek, who had been watching the children for her, I noticed the display of my photographs of Baby Jonathan on the wall, over a shelf holding his baby bottle and teddy bear. "That's my shrine to Jonathan," Carol said quietly, and we stood together for a while, remembering. As it turned out, my pictures were the only ones the family had of this baby—no one ever thought he would have only six weeks of life. On another wall, I noticed a group of photographs of Carol's many godchildren.

A small child came to the door just then with a note in her hand. Carol gently invited her in and took the paper from her hand.

Dear Carol,

Please can we have some bread I won't ask for anything else. Because I can pay you when I get my food stamps at any price you ask. I just been crying I can't handle not have anything to feed them.

I know it's no one fault but my own and I've never done this type of thing before. If you can just help me I will never let you be a shame of anything I ever do again. I'll see you Monday because I'm shame for what I'm going through. I'll get help this week. Please help.

A few minutes later, a different child came with another note.

Please Carol help me I have nobody else to turn to please help me just for today. They haven't had anything since early yesterday. I won't every ask again. I sorry for keep bugging you. You're the only one that can help me.

A few days after these notes were written, both families were evicted.

Homeless

My first involvement with homeless people came in November 1985 when one of the women I had been photographing in Carol's building told me there was a place in Newark where whole families were living outside in the weeds. On a warm November afternoon I went with her brother, Tyrone, to see if I could find out something about how these people survived.

As we drove up I saw six men sitting on crates in a garbage-filled vacant lot. My heart sank. I pushed past my fear, and we made our way through the debris to the group. I asked them whether they would be willing to tell me what it was like to live there. All refused except one, Arthur, who was known on the street as "Diamond" (p. 27).

Diamond led us around an area marked off by a broken-down fence and explained that this was where the people slept. There were nineteen of them. He said that the fence and their dog had given them some protection from outsiders. But now everything was in a shambles. It seems that on the previous day someone had vandalized their place while they were out looking for food. Only remnants were left of the steel drum they had used for cooking. The dog had been hanged from the tree, the small propane refrigerator stolen, and the crates and tables broken up. Diamond and three others in the homeless group who now joined us were close to tears as they described what they had lost and how they had lived.

In this fenced-off area, each person had had a private space sectioned off from the others by large, flat pieces of cardboard. Every day they would comb the city for food and firewood, some returning with a few carrots and potatoes and scraps of wood. The ones who returned empty-handed had to do the cooking and the cleaning up. "We were never full, but we were okay," said Diamond. "Now we have to look for an abandoned car or a hole to crawl into when the sun starts to go down." The city tore down the abandoned house where they used to stay when the weather was bad.

As the others drifted away, Diamond told us something about his life. He was a licensed barber who had gotten into trouble and served time. But after he got out of jail no one would hire him.

Most of us got burned out of our place to live [Diamond explained]. Friends or relatives can only take you in for so long before you got to go. Some are homeless from a combination of things. One person lost a good-payin' job and couldn't find another equal in pay. Even three small jobs wasn't enough to keep the house and the car. Then the family broke up, and then the spirit is lost, and here they are—women, men, and children.

We sleep in abandoned cars and empty buildings and in somebody's hallway, because we don't have a place of our own. When you don't have a place of your own, you have to deal with the superintendent or whoever they are that tell you that you have to get up and out of where you're sleepin'. They say, "What you doin' here!" "Well," you say, "I'm restin'." "Rest somewhere else. Don't rest here." So I got to go.

"Most of the people who are living like this look away when they run into someone they know," Diamond said. "I'm not just against the wall, I'm in it. It's real bad. This is not the movies or television. This is real."

As we were leaving, Tyrone got into the car while I took a couple of photographs. In a blur, I saw a woman with a box knife running toward me screaming about her "rights." Diamond headed her off as she continued to express her outrage at me for taking her picture without permission. I apologized profusely for not asking her first, as I usually do. But I hadn't noticed her because she was so far away. Nervously repeating, "You're right, you're right," I slid into my car and drove away.

A few years after this interview, the city put cyclone fences around the vacant lots. I called city hall and was told that the fences were not to keep out homeless people, but to keep people from throwing garbage into the lots. The following week, city officials using bull horns announced from moving vehicles that fire barrels would no longer be allowed. As a result, people would no longer take the scrap wood that I brought them because now they feared being arrested for making fires. At the same time, the abandoned cars in which some people had been living were towed away.

In 1977, when I began documenting poverty on the Lower East Side of Manhattan, homelessness was relatively uncommon. By 1980, a growing number of people were living on the streets. Shelters sprang up in response to the crisis. The people running the shelters were overwhelmed, not just by the increased numbers who checked in every night, but by the numbers they had to turn away. Thelma, a woman who worked at one of the shelters in Newark, said that it's much easier to tell people on the telephone that there isn't any space available than it is to turn away a mother and baby standing at the door in rain or snow. "That's really hard."

In 1986, while preparing an article, I spent several months researching homelessness in Newark and interviewing various officials. It enabled me to get a sense of what was going on in the world of people without homes. For the policymakers, it was a time of transition; a new administration was coming in and many were insecure about their jobs, which may be why people didn't feel able to commit themselves to doing something about the homeless problem. They were extremely courteous and seemed very concerned, but nothing was ever accomplished.

In fact, as part of that investigation in 1986 I made many unsuccessful telephone calls to the chair of the task force on housing in Newark. When I finally got through to her, she said, "We haven't looked at the homeless situation yet." She said she wanted to learn more about the problem and asked me to send her information collected for a shelter program proposal that I had written, along with others' proposals. She never acknowledged receiving our materials. Five years later, several shelter directors told me that this person had never called a single meeting of the community leaders actively involved with the homeless.

"The 'Y' is willing to expand this shelter program," said Verna Morgan, director of the YM-YWCA's homeless program, "but public officials say there is no money for renovation. However, Newark has spent, and continues to spend, hundreds of thousands of dollars to house the homeless temporarily at the Lincoln Motel for $50 a night."

Now, I understand, the taxpayers are giving the motel $67 a night for the same purpose. Almost a billion dollars has been spent in the past few years for these motels, Verna Morgan told me, "and we get pennies." Many leaders working on this problem agree that money now earmarked for these motels would be better spent on permanent shelter: low-income housing, single-room occupancy buildings, and roominghouses.

Housing is scarce in Newark. There is a − 1 percent vacancy rate for affordable housing, which is substandard, and decent housing is just too expensive. The going rate for a two-bedroom apartment in the ghetto is $600. After trying to help a nineteen-year-old mother find an apartment for herself and her child, Verna Morgan concluded that it was impossible to locate a place she could afford. "The space at the shelter," she said, "is all this woman has."

"It appears the only plan the city has is, 'Let's create homelessness,'" commented Hector Rodriques, housing coordinator of La Casa de Don Pedro, a community organization. "It's called gentrification, and since many of the Hispanics are renters, they have fear of displacement." To be sure, there is no policy to end homelessness, and as Don Jackson, a former director of St. Rocco's Community Outreach Center, pointed out, "Until they sit down and work out a plan for single homeless people, it's helter-skelter. Send the homeless here, send them there, fourteen days to Fulton Street, send them to St. Rocco's, send them to welfare, welfare refers them back to St. Rocco's. It's a round-robin kind of thing, and the people aren't helped."

Not since the Great Depression of the 1930s have so many women, men, and children been homeless in the United States. It is not possible to make an accurate count, but estimates range from seven hundred thousand to three million. According to the Coalition for the Homeless in Washington, D.C., the number is growing at a rate of about 20 percent a year. In Newark, a city official said, off the record, that early in 1992 the official count of people without homes was twenty-three thousand. This number included people who were doubling up and waiting for services.

Relatively few of today's homeless are the stereotypical Skid Row derelicts or bag ladies. In the past decade the fastest-growing segment of people without a permanent home is families with children. Karen Olson, director of the Interfaith Hospitality Network in Summit, New Jersey, estimates that they now make up about 40 percent of this population. "We also see working families who are homeless," she told me. "One or two in the family are working, and they still cannot afford housing."

This predicament is especially traumatic for children. Their parents and people who work with homeless children say youngsters need only experience a day or two without shelter before they need counseling. Being homeless shatters their sense of security. Often they feel humiliated as well. Several children have told me that they ask the driver of the school bus from the shelter to drop them off a few blocks away from school so the other students won't find out that they live in a shelter.

Rod Austin's job at the Newark Board of Education is to make sure that when children become homeless and have to go to a shelter, they are not removed from their original school if they change districts. "It's enough to experience being burned out of one's home without having to switch schools as well. But maybe an aunt or a grandparent still lives in the neighborhood, and the child can stay with them for a while. Or we can provide the child with bus tickets even if the shelter is far from the school. The main thing is to keep some stability in children's lives."

Families need to stay together when they are in crisis. But the first thing most shelters do is to separate the parents. The children go with the mother. If there is a male child over fourteen, he will go with the father. I know of families who stay in cars rather than go to a shelter where they will be split up.

Our political leaders still place this crisis low on their agenda. HUD's budget for building low-income housing has been cut 75 percent in the past ten years, and this has created a situation where there are two low-income renters for each unit available, according to Karen Olson.

"I call it survival of the fittest," she said. "Because the ones least able to compete are on the street. The elderly, the disabled, the single mothers working as nurses' aides, teachers' aides, clerks—they're working, but they cannot afford housing. Even substandard housing is difficult to find."

Some years ago, I made it a practice to take my high school classes to visit homeless shelters in Newark. My students were surprised to see how articulate and polite people who live in shelters are. They saw how confining these places are. It shocked them to see beds lined up next to each other, almost touching. And they were amazed to learn that the residents cannot just come and go as they please. Losing their freedom and privacy is something they had never even thought about.

This experience stayed with some students for many years. Not long ago, I was invited back to the high school by one of these students. She had started a volunteer group to help in homeless shelters and asked if I would give a talk to the group. Over the years, as I came to know my students, I realized that many of them seem to be bored living in the suburbs because there's so little to do. But as soon as they become involved in something meaningful, they come alive.

After taking a trip to Newark with some high school students to see my exhibit on the Central Ward in a gallery there, then to visit a shelter, I recorded the following comments:

> I thought the trip to Newark was *outstanding*. The one word I feel sums up the whole trip is the word "raw." There was no cover-up of what happens or what is actually there. What I saw really reached me and touched me. There were no doctors with five Ph.D.s telling you what drugs and alcohol do to you. There were *real* people who had used drugs and had lived out what the results were. Seeing with one's own eyes what was there hits you like a concrete block. One does not know the words to describe what he feels or what he sees. I started laughing as I entered the building. Not because there was anything funny but there was an uncomfortable feeling. I did not know if I should laugh or cry. It was scary, entering from one world to another world, yet knowing I was in the same world, yet different levels. I can't describe what I learned because I learned with my heart and not with my mind. I admit I was afraid of them because I really was. Not that they were going to hurt me but because they were something I had known nothing about. Anyway I learned a lot

and the trip opened my mind as well as my heart. Thank you for the experience of seeing firsthand what is really there. I admire you for what you do and how much you care.

The picture exhibit was also *excellent*. The pictures gave off an aura that made your eyes stay with the picture. The eyes and faces of the children were so innocent, so clear, yet the environment behind them was so bleak. It captured what is really there and what those kids have to do to live in that environment. It is definitely not conducive to their life. The trip was an incredible experience, one that I feel I will never forget.

When our class visited a homeless shelter for men, it really wasn't like I expected it to be. I pictured a place where men would be lying around, and lots of noise and confusion. There were six men who stayed and talked to the class. The shelter is closed from nine to five. All of the men had the same problem. All the men became mixed up with the wrong group as teenagers. Drugs and alcohol played an important part in their lives.

Through this direct experience, the students learned how limiting stereotyping is, not only to its victims, but to everyone else. It interferes with thinking clearly about a problem like homelessness. And it cuts people off from each other—and from the enrichment that comes from exposure to different people.

According to Susan Baker, chair of the National Alliance to End Homelessness, "We have to teach compassion. If we don't expose children to the problems of the world and to other children like themselves, their own age, who come from different environments, they may not outgrow their childhood biases."[1]

1. *What You Can Do to Teach the Homeless* (New York: Simon and Schuster, 1991), p. 63.

Rasheek and his cousin
sharing junking money,
October 1985

Chapter 3
Survivin'

► ► ►

K eeping a roof over your head is obviously essential to protecting yourself and your children. But in the Central Ward
it is becoming increasingly difficult as the supply of housing
shrinks. When I first saw Rebecca, she and her husband were living
with their five children on the third floor of a house across the street
from Carol's building. On a freezing January day, her husband, John,
walked me through the house, which had just been listed as abandoned. A broken water pipe on the first floor had flooded the entire
downstairs, and it was slick with ice. In the ice-covered bathroom,
water was still pouring in. Heavy icicles hung from the kitchen ceiling. It was the most eerie sight I had ever seen.

In Rebecca and John's apartment, the only heat came from the
gas jets on the stove. They were desperately trying to find another
place to live. Each time they went out to work or in search of rooms,
a neighbor or one of the older children would sit behind the door for
them, holding a bat to protect their meager belongings. A couple of
weeks later, the place caught on fire. Now homeless, they were housed
in the Lincoln Motel.

Generally, poor families do not have much of a networking system to fall back on when an emergency occurs. Many turn to whatever
social agencies are available, others return to the state they originally
came from. Some give up. An emergency housing official later told me
that after six years of trying to make it in New Jersey, Rebecca and her
family had moved back to Georgia.

Being burned out is not the only threat; parents on welfare with
small children must also worry about whether their apartment will
pass inspection by the social worker. Parents, rather than landlords,
are often punished for housing code violations, as happened to Carol's
neighbor Angie before she moved into Carol's building. Angie's social
worker told her that her apartment was an unfit place to bring up children and that if she didn't move within a month, they would be put
into a foster home. So Angie frantically accumulated enough money
for one-and-one-half months' rent and a month's security, plus moving expenses, and had to find a better apartment—this in a housing

market with a vacancy rate under 1 percent. Later she managed to find a place in Carol's building.

Many violations of the building code are recorded by inspectors. But, according to Newark councilman George Branch, some landlords get off easier than others—it depends on the judge. Countless times over the years, after the landlord of a particular building found out that I was photographing the falling ceilings, the window frames without glass, the exposed wiring, and many other violations, repairs were miraculously made. I recall one such time being devastated over the condition of a certain apartment building and telling the tenants that I would come back in two days with a video camera. I returned to find the broken skylight fixed, the garbage gone, and the place looking generally better. There were also times when I phoned the authorities to complain that the people didn't have any heat, and a few hours later it was restored. When the tenants themselves call, they often have to wait weeks for a response. The heat might stay on for only a few hours or for a day, and then the tenants will be told by the landlord that the boiler is broken or that there is no oil. One tenant told me that the landlord puts in only fifty gallons of oil at a time. Mostly, however, people don't complain, because with a complaint they must leave their name and run the risk of being evicted. As bad as it is, it is still a roof over their heads.

"Nothing lasts that the landlord fixes here," says Carol. "Why would a landlord even want a place if he didn't want to keep it up? If they're not making money, why would they be here? I guess if it falls down, he writes it off his taxes. If it burns up, he gets the insurance money. So what's he losing? He sure ain't worryin' about the heat. As for fixin' things, they use the cheapest stuff and put it up any old way. They barely out the door and the plaster is already fallin' down. They say we don't take care of it."

Of course, some tenants leave the apartments damaged, thus increasing the landlord's problems. People who do this tend to be either habitually destructive or angry about having to pay high rent for a "rat hole." The new tenants are the ones that suffer. They have to deal with the mess knowing that it is a major struggle to get anything fixed. This happened to Mary, a young woman who used to live on the second floor in Carol's building. The landlord promised her that the bathroom sink and tub would be fixed as soon as she moved in. Not only did the fixtures remain useless, but the bathroom ceiling fell in.

In addition to having to cope with violations, tenants experience constant anxiety over not knowing from one day to the next what plans are in store for their building, and how these plans will affect them and their families. One day, everyone in Carol's building was told that it was being sold and they would all be evicted. Another day, they were told the building was condemned. Still another time, the landlord said the building was going under Section Eight (meaning rents would be subsidized by HUD), and everyone should go downtown and fill out Section Eight applications. Later it was announced that everyone's rent was going to be raised because the landlord was planning to remodel the building. The work began, but after a few months it stopped. The latest word is that the landlord is trying to sell the building.

Crisis came knocking on the door one day while I was talking to Carol. Because the fan and the television were on, I could hear only her response to the landlord who stood in the doorway.

What do you mean he has nothing to do with this building? We've been payin' him the rent for the past six months. You're putting the people in the middle of your battle. That ain't right. You're like a stranger to these people. Now you want the people to just give you the rent? You come with him and tell the people there's a change. Come *together* and tell the people. Put it in writing—have it notarized. Three different owners! They don't know who to pay the rent to, and then you say they could be evicted. Out of the blue sky you say you want the rent. The people need some proof.

After he left, Carol said, "He gonna mess up the tenants, and I'm not gonna let that happen." I asked Carol to repeat the entire conversation, using letters instead of names because I couldn't keep it straight. Even with letters it is not easy. Carol told it as follows:

> We have a mortgage holder, *A,* a deed holder, *B,* and a manager, *C.* They all consider themselves owners.
>
> *A* said *B* holds the deed, but don't hold the mortgage papers. *A* holds the mortgage papers. *A* says *B* is supposed to pay him $1,300 every month until he gets $90,000. Then *A* will give *B* the mortgage papers.
>
> But *B* stopped paying *A* for the mortgage papers. Before *B* stopped paying *A,* he hired *C. C* came in and told everybody he was the new owner. In reality, he was just the manager for *B. C* put a lot of his own money in the building, according to what he told us, because he holds the right to manage, with the right to buy.
>
> *A* got mad at *B* because *B* stopped paying on the mortgage papers. So *A* looked into the contract and found out if *B* stopped paying on the mortgage paper then *A* had the right to collect the rent directly, 'cause *B* forfeited his right to collect the money. But since *C* collects the money, he said *A* don't have a right 'cause he has the right from *B.*
>
> *C* tells me *A* has no right to the rent money. *A* tells me *C* has no right, period.
>
> *A* says he's taking over the property, which leaves out *B* and *C.* But the majority of the tenants, who have been here for the past seven months, have leases with *C.*
>
> *A* said he's gonna send out papers telling all the tenants to pay him the rent money.
>
> *C* says if the tenants pay *A,* they're still obligated to pay him and can be taken to court and evicted.
>
> *A* says if they don't pay him, he's gonna take them to court and have them evicted.

Later, when we were alone, Carol said,

I have something that I didn't tell you because I was too ashamed. But I was so desperate to move that I answered an ad in the paper for a five-room apartment for $275 a month, including heat, hot water, and no security. When I contacted the office, the woman said to bring in $160 and we will get you an apartment. They suppose to contact landlords for you, but I'm waiting almost nine months for the apartment that's still advertised in the paper. When I call every day, they say the apartment is still vacant and the owner will contact you. I don't know what is going on. It's written on my receipt that it is a lifetime service, so I can't get my money back. It'll take that long for them to find my apartment. Now I got to pay back my sister and mother, and I'm still here.

On September 19, 1991, using my own name, I answered the same newspaper ad: "Newark 5 rooms $275/mo." The man said it was no longer available. (No business name was given.)

I called Carol and told her what the man had said. Earlier she had called the same number, and "Al" had claimed that the apartment would be available on the first of the month. But every time she calls he changes the date to a later one. He had given Carol a special number that went straight to the rental part of the office. When I called the special number, the same man answered, this time saying, "Apartments Unlimited." He said he was Al, and I said I was Carol. He told me the apartment would be available on the first of the month and to keep in touch. Carol has been calling since January 4, 1991, without success.

She has been on the waiting list for public housing for eight years.

Unskilled work that pays enough to support a family is probably hard to find anywhere, but in the largest city in New Jersey, it is almost impossible. Even a good education doesn't always guarantee a suitable job. Carol's cousin had a college degree and was only able to get work as a clerk-typist in a local hospital.

Being on welfare is not the answer. "Your life is not your own," said Carol. "You have to answer for everything." It's dehumanizing. People want to work.

Mary, who is nineteen, signed up for business school in 1991. She had to take out a $1,246 loan for the six-month course, but the $41 a month she had to pay on top of that for a bus ticket had her borrowing from everyone she could. She told me she wanted her children to have better than she had. Not to struggle so much. "Welfare keeps you poor," she said. Then one day in October Mary came home crying. It seems the computer/bookkeeping class had been canceled because there weren't enough students. She had recently arranged for a young woman to babysit in exchange for room and board.

The unemployment rate in the ghetto has long been much higher than the country's norm, usually hovering around 50 percent. The shift from a manufacturing to a service economy helped push the rate up to this level. Service jobs for which unskilled workers are eligible tend to pay the minimum wage or below, and most lack benefits. The main problem with taking a minimum-wage job paying $202 for a forty-hour week and giving up welfare is that it could mean losing one's medical benefits and jeopardize the family's access to Medicaid—and the job could turn out to be temporary.

Despite the fact that minimum-wage jobs pay $5.05 an hour, yielding an income 20 percent below the poverty line for a family of three, people I know in the Central Ward still try to get work. Carol, while studying to get her G.E.D. certificate, said, "I thought I was too old to go back to school, but at twenty-nine, I am the youngest woman in the class. There are twelve others; one is fifty-nine. They talk about how happy they are that they finally got their chance to go back to school."

Sitting in Carol's kitchen one day, I listened as the talk turned to work. One neighbor pointed out that people often have difficulty communicating with employers. "Don't forget," she explained, "being on welfare you can't afford a phone. The bosses can't call you back or call you in. You don't have the money to constantly call them." People in the Central Ward have to rely on street pay phones.

"You don't have transportation," said another. "No money to pay the bus fare. If I got a job today, how would I get there? How would I dress? I ain't got no money to buy decent clothes." It's a Catch-22 situation.

Joann had a job for seven years, pressing clothes. "I was one with that machine," she said. "I loved that job. But then I got hit by a car that never stopped. Now I can only stand for short periods of time. My body is all wrong. Now I'm looking for a part-time job, something where I don't have to stand."

Keeping a job can be as difficult as finding one. Glen (p. 51), who supports a wife and four small children, walked each day to his mattress factory job, and at night he drew antidrug posters for local businesses. The last time I saw him he had applied to the local art school, hoping to become involved with computer art. But more recently I heard that the factory was closing.

After years of commuting into the ghetto, I have not found many situations where unskilled people had the opportunity to pull themselves up. What I did find were situations where they were constantly being pushed down. Rasheek's struggle to find a better way to live reflects this kind of experience.

"I was the only one to graduate high school, out of the six kids," Rasheek told me, "and always wanted to do better for myself."

> I got my first job through my father when I was sixteen, working on a garbage truck. School and working is what I did. After school I worked, and then I did my homework. At nineteen I got involved in street life—I started drinking.
>
> Every job I get always goes just so far and something happens—some kind of an excuse to get rid of me. It's been ten years, but they won't stop me. After the garbage truck job, I worked in the recycling places in Newark. I never got any benefits and every week for the entire year my paycheck always came

up short. I explained it to my foreman, but he never translated the message to the big boss. I had to deal with it because I had a wife and children that depended on me. One day I spoke up to the big boss. I told him how I worked forty hours and was only paid for thirty or twenty-nine or twenty-eight hours. One time I even worked ten hours overtime and my week's check was $7.35—they made me wait for the rest of my pay for two weeks. In front of the big boss, the foreman struck me and I struck him back and was fired. I stopped drinking almost a year now. After that, I enrolled in a six-month government course that paid me $200 a week (no benefits) to learn how to demolish buildings. I got the highest evaluations. After six months they make you wait another three before they give you the certificate to get a job in that field. I had to look for something else because people are depending on me.

So I applied for a job at the mall that just opened in my neighborhood. They gave me a position in the deli department, cutting meats and making sandwiches. The market makes you wait six months before you are allowed into the union, then another three months before you begin to receive any benefits—nothing is guaranteed during that time. The hours you work are always different; each week they post a new schedule. Sometimes it's thirty-five hours, sometimes twenty-seven. If they let me, I would work sixty hours.

After a month and a half, I was on a trial period for becoming the night supervisor for the deli. They told me, of all the other guys, I was the only worker they could count on.

Then one day I went to work and found out that someone had accused me of stealing six bags of Pampers. The store called the cops and had me arrested. Some old drunk who was hired to sweep the walks said he's not sure, but I look like the guy. The cops came and put handcuffs on me—took me to the precinct. They checked me and found out I had a clean record. They fingerprinted me. It was six hours before they released me. They gave me a court date for the theft charge. They fired me and I'm now barred from the store.

Three days later I talked to the security guard and he told me he caught the guys who stole the Pampers. I asked him why they are still pressing charges against me. He said, "Because the drunk said he seen you."

I went to my court arraignment on February 7. I pled not guilty. I filed for a public defender. The judge set the court date for April 3. The public defender told me that I wasn't allowed to talk to him until a week before the court date.

In the meantime I'm out of work. I can't get another job until I clear my name. So I'm right back picking up cans and taking them to the recycling place. I'm not drinking. But I feel cheated—and used. When there was no one there to work I came in and worked for them and now they can't take my word. They also fired my co-worker because she stood up for me. I would love to know what happened to her.

On April 3, Rasheek met me as I walked into the courthouse. "My name was not called on the roll," he said,

so I had to go to the third floor to the public defender's office. He said to go down to 212. At 212 he said to go to "that window." At that window I told the clerk my name and it came up in the computer—the charge came up: "receiving stolen goods." Since they changed the charge from *stealing* goods to *receiving* stolen goods, they changed my public defender. The one I had only deals with stealing goods, not receiving stolen goods. Don't ask me the difference. The clerk said my court date was changed to April 30. Everything for today has been canceled out. Just like that. I just started a new job working by the day at a recycling place, and already I had to take time off. My wife and son came to help me in court if I needed it, and you came to give support, all for nothing.

They knew this charge was changed two weeks ago. Why

couldn't they send me a letter? Why did we all have to come down here today? This system is all messed up. I told my boss I'd be in late. So I lost time and money. They're gonna keep going back and forth and keep changing the court date and the charge.

Then they're gonna end up throwing it out—but that doesn't take it off my record. They will just dismiss the charge. You're guilty until you're proven innocent. I won't be proven innocent because they will dismiss the charge. So when I go for a job and they check my record, it's still there. I would have to sue the people who have made false charges against me in order to clear my name. I don't have the time or money to do that.

A few weeks later, the charges were thrown out of court.

On another occasion, a job was interrupted for the boss's convenience. Rasheek was told to go home because his employer had to go to the hospital for a couple of weeks. "No pay. No nothing. Just like that," he recalls.

Injury on the job can also be a serious problem because people on temporary employment often are not protected. One time, the bucket on the side of the bobcat ran over Rasheek's foot. I saw him with his swollen foot, barely able to hobble around. He was sure the company would pay him for the time he had to stay home. Instead they told him there were no benefits and if he expected any, not to come back.

"Junking" is all too often a mainstay of economic survival in this area. It is a way of making money by collecting aluminum, stainless steel, brass, and copper from lots, streets, and garbage cans. Using a shopping cart with milk crates tied to it, it is possible to make $10 for a ten-hour day.

But Carol doesn't want her son to junk. I found that interesting because in the suburbs most children are encouraged to get a paper route, which I guess would be the equivalent of junking. After a while I realized there was a big difference between the two jobs. In the suburbs no one thinks one's children will deliver newspapers when they grow up. Certainly that is not what the parents do. But in the ghetto there is a very real possibility that the children *will* grow up to junk— to imitate what they see, follow their parents.

Relatively fit men can sometimes pick up day work doing various menial jobs. Vans come by from all over looking for cheap labor. The photograph of Joe (p. 32) makes it look as if he's not working. The truth of the matter is, he is waiting for the van to come and pick him up and take him to a job as a plumber's helper. In the suburbs, if people are sitting outside, it's assumed they're on vacation. But in the ghetto, men sitting around are automatically thought to be lazy.

Joe had four or five jobs at factories that either burned down or moved out of Newark. Lacking transportation to follow these firms, he joined the National Guard and was injured; he now receives partial disability. He wants to get his plumber's license, but he can't afford to go to school and work at the same time—to "keep the wheel a turnin' to keep budgeted up in life," he says. "So we sit here in the summer and by the barrel in the winter, waitin' for the first job to come by so we can grab it. If we sit in the house we're not goin' to get no job."

Another aspect of the struggle to find work appears in the many stories about people living in drug areas who go to jail because someone falsely accuses them of selling drugs. And in this time of anti-drug hysteria the accused are often roughed up, humiliated, forced to spend weeks in jail—longer if they are not eligible for the bail program. The community bail program will lend money to people who don't have the resources. Twenty-year-old Robert, who was arrested after being accused of selling drugs, told me, "At least I'm out of jail, even though I owe the bail money. I keep trying to get a job, but they just say, 'We'll call you.' They never do. I went to the Job Corps in Kentucky and received a certificate to lay bricks and still I cannot find a job." On top of everything he now has a court appearance coming up, but he was never told who accused him of doing what he says he never did. Being suspected of a crime can be as devastating to one's future as being convicted.

Carol was furious when Robert finished his story. "The majority of the young black boys are just glad they got out of jail," she fumed. "They don't realize they had their rights taken away, and was stripped of their pride. All they look at is they're out and free, that they got home—instead of looking at the whole thing being wrong from the beginning."

Where work is concerned, mothers often run into a dilemma that is especially painful. They are pushed to get a job and are heavily stigmatized if they collect welfare. But if they are out working and their children are not properly taken care of, the Division of Youth and Family Services (DYFS) will remove the children and put them into foster homes.

Gloria wishes she had never told welfare that she was working. Although she knew her grant would stop, the authorities told her she could still count on being eligible for food stamps. But two months after going off welfare, she still had not received her stamps. On top of that, the guidance office called to say that her eleven- and twelve-year-old children were not always attending school, so they were going to call DYFS. Since Gloria had to leave the house to go to work at 5:30 in the morning, she had placed her eighteen-year-old daughter in charge, and it turned out that the teenager had not looked after them properly. Finally, threatened with the loss of her younger children, Gloria quit her job.

Now Gloria is back where she started. She can't afford to pay for someone to watch the children and she can't leave them because they are under age thirteen and not allowed to be in the house by themselves. "My nosy neighbors will also call DYFS if my kids are alone, so I guess I'm right back on welfare again."

Finding reliable child care is the special problem that all mothers have when they go out to work. Often, in days gone by, women relied on their mothers. But in the ghetto many grandmothers are too depressed or sick to care for children. Carol's mother, for instance, is incapacitated by the consequences of diabetes. Diana's mother had a colostomy and is severely depressed.

Alicia, a high school graduate, had a similar predicament. She loved working in an office and had an offer from Bradlee's department store to be a bookkeeper. They were even willing to supply her with transportation. So she had her mother move in to take care of her two children. But her mother drank so much that Alicia had to take care of her instead. She also asked the father of her children if he would watch them while she went to work, since he couldn't find a job. He said he would take care of one child but not two. A short time later, they had an argument and he ripped out the fuse boxes from the building. The landlord then evicted Alicia, her children, and her mother.

In the ghetto, needing to protect one's children and not always being able to do so can give you nightmares. There is the constant worry that children will be violated outdoors or even in their own households. Angie told me that she stopped working and went back on welfare because her six-year-old daughter was raped. She decided she wasn't going to leave the child alone again until she could take care of herself.

Chapter 4
No easy walk
► ► ►

Annie, Sidney, and Tamika in "Hoodlum City" (Stella Wright, a high-rise public housing project in the Central Ward of Newark), December 1985. Criminals use abandoned apartments on the first floor for pistol practice and for taking dope

▼
▼
▼

A t Carol's kitchen table one day, she and I talked about the health worries in her community. Looking at the photographs I had brought with me, she lingered over the one of Jonathan, the baby who died (p. 69). "Can you talk a little about the baby?" I asked. Her lips started quivering. "Maybe some other time," I suggested. "That might be better," she said,

(p. 69)

> because lately I have been thinking a lot about the baby. That baby gave me back my life. The tragedy with that baby gave us a different life. It made me realize that I could wake up one morning and my whole house could be gone. At first I denied it. It took a while to stop drinking and get my house in order. That child gave me the strength. I gave him birth, but he gave me life. The Lord had to touch my heart. It made me realize my kids were more important than that bottle of wine.
>
> The wake made me realize that the baby died. The people there were sorry, but they were dancing and drinking and laughing like everything was still the same. But, it wasn't the same for me. Later, I realized I had to change, not the people.

Another time, Carol told me about Baby Jonathan's death.

> Once a month, I never drank the two days before I had to go to the welfare board. The board didn't put up with smelling alcohol on your breath 'cause they come get your kids. This particular time, when Jonathan was six weeks old, I had a Monday morning appointment. So I didn't drink. I cleaned the apartment, washed and ironed the kids' clothes for school. I gave Jonathan a bottle and at eleven-thirty Jonathan was still playing in his chair with the angels. That's what I say when babies be smiling and looking up at the ceiling waving their arms and stuff. Anyway, I was playin' with Jonathan, he was just laughin'. I told him to stop playin' with the angels 'cause it's time for you to go to sleep. I made my sandwich, and a cup of soda and looked in the chair and saw he was fallin' asleep. So I lay Jonathan down in his bed.

I ate my sandwich and went to sleep. The next morning he was gone. When the police came in they looked around, everything was in place. They seen the children's clothes neatly laid out. They said right away, "This is a crib death." I often think, suppose it was the other way around, suppose I was drunk and the house was a mess. I just thank God, 'cause a lot of times you drink alcohol you just don't know what's done, not done. I could have lost all my kids, not just the one.

Carol stayed drunk for a month, "tryin' to drink away pain that wasn't goin' anywhere." Then one Sunday she woke up and something kept telling her to go to church. She had not been to church since she was a child. Instead, she rolled over and pulled the sheets over her head, but the sense that she had to go to church persisted.

She got up, washed, and dressed just as Rasheek came back from the store where he had gone to buy milk and cereal for the kids' breakfast. He was surprised and asked her where she was going. "To church!"

I didn't know where I was goin'. I was just walkin' down the street and there was a big, ol' stone church on the corner. I went to go up those stairs, and I seen this little store-front church across the street. I walked over there and thought I was late, everybody was gone. It was empty. I sat down in the back and dusted off my Bible. Just then the pastor came out, followed by a woman and two children who sat in the front row. Church started. I was lookin' around waitin' for everybody else to come in—where everybody at? After the opening prayers the pastor got up and started preachin' about livin' in sin, knowin' you know there is a God. How people be drinkin' and partyin' and how God had a better way for you, for your life. He went on and I knew he was preachin' my life to me. I kinda looked around—there was nobody else there. I couldn't believe he was talkin' to me. You know how sometimes people be talkin' to you and you take it personal?

He didn't know me. I knew it was God talkin' to me through this man. He kept sayin', "I don't know why God got me goin' down this road 'cause this ain't the sermon I planned for today. But I'm gonna preach it anyhow." He kept sayin' and talkin' about runnin' in your house for comfort and there's so much goin' on inside your house, you run outside and there's nothin' out there. I thought about that. How many times we had a house full of people and nobody listened to me when I told them to shut up all that noise, my kids were tryin' to sleep and didn't need to hear that. So I went outside the door and all my friends was out there drinkin' and carryin' on. So I ran back inside. And the preacher said, "You run out for comfort and come in for comfort and find no comfort." I knew that man was talkin' to me! "God will bring a dramatic thing in your life that will turn you around. Just like runnin' for comfort there will just be brick walls and God will corner you among those brick walls and turn your life around."

I thought about the dramatic thing that happened in my life. It was waking up one day and my baby wasn't there, and that's what he was talkin' about. I was tryin' to seek comfort and couldn't find any.

After service let out, I left real fast. I didn't want nobody say nothin' to me. I got across the street, I actually had to sit down on this corner thing there and take a breather. God! I know you was talkin' to me. I got home and poured the wine and beer down the drain and told my kids next week we're all goin' to church. And next Sunday we all stood up in front of the church.

I know for a fact that Jonathan, my baby, came to give me life. I was dead in life. Everything in the house was dead. Everything was goin' wrong. I birthed him, but he gave me life. He died and in his death, I came alive. Not only did he give it to me but he gave it to my kids. There was a reason he was born and his job was done when he came, and when he passed he was finished.

I didn't really want Jonathan when I got pregnant. I had three kids, but abortion was like out the family rules. I can remember holding Jonathan one night, he was cryin' and I was drunk and shook him and said, "Won't you go back where you came from?" Then I put him to bed and maybe two weeks after that he passed. I always felt guilty about that. I believed I sent him back. Now knowing how God works I understand things that you say can come back to you. Now I know 'cause God told me when I was prayin' that Jonathan came to give us life. If my baby didn't come and die of crib death what would happen?

I used to try and stop drinking and my friends would laugh and say, "We'll give you until this afternoon. You be reachin' out that window." I could go two days and that was it. But after church each day was easier and easier to do. My friends were still drinking, still offering it to me, but it just wasn't there. Like what is that suppose to do. I know that God did that for me. Since I went to Christ he took the taste of alcohol out of my mouth.

Another time, still thinking about the high rate of sickness and death in the ghetto, Carol reflected that just last week a tenant on the fourth floor had told her that her niece, who was pregnant, had recently died from measles. The unborn child died with her. "I didn't know you could die from measles," Carol commented. She added that two months ago a baby on the third floor had died. The family was without heat for two weeks. The baby caught cold and kept getting worse. She was in the hospital for a month, but no one was able to save her.

Rashes are another problem in this area. Scabies. Doctors haven't heard about scabies in years. It seems that the children pick up these rashes when they play in empty lots contaminated by rodents. The parents call it a dirt rash. Mothers say the children also get rashes from the water—the pipes are rusted and rotted. Eye infections are rampant too.

Sickness is common year round in the Central Ward. There always seem to be colds, ear infections, stomach viruses, sore throats. It is not unusual to finish with one virus and start another.

The percentage of people with AIDS in Newark is second only to that in New York City. Parents are very frightened, worried their children will catch this disease. "Years before we would let the kids have things from other folks, share their soda or lick the lollipops, but no more," said Carol. In addition to AIDS, parents worry about gonorrhea and syphilis—even, in recent years, about tuberculosis and measles. Low birthweight, injuries, abuse, and preventable diseases are especially common, as they are among the poor elsewhere. Lead poisoning is widespread in the Central Ward because the district has so many old buildings. The New Jersey State Department of Health estimated in 1991 that 28,592 children under five years of age had dangerous levels of lead in their bodies, and Newark has the worst lead poisoning problem in New Jersey.

As we talked in the hot, dark kitchen and more women squeezed into the tiny room, I was thankful for the breeze from the fan. Years ago, I had brought it to Rasheek from a neighborhood cleanup because he'd said he could fix anything. One woman described how she worried about the children falling on glass, metal, and nails, and others chimed in. Debris is everywhere.

Another neighbor mentioned the problem with rats. "I have to stay up all night to watch that rats don't bite my children," she said. "If I doze off, I wake with a start, I see the rats, and I cry and scream." Still another woman told about the time she woke up to find a rat standing on its hind legs looking at her. She ran from the building screaming, "Let them have the house! Let them have it!"

I left Carol's for a time and went upstairs to photograph four-year-old Danielle, whose family had just moved in. They had told me they didn't have any pictures of her. As I framed the child's old and serious face in my viewfinder and brought her into focus, I could only go on by telling myself, surely, if I can convey what I am seeing to others, this suffering will not be allowed to continue. The child stood before me quietly. I desperately tried to record what I saw. After photographing Danielle, I asked if she was hungry. She whispered, "Yes." I took her back to Carol's apartment, where we gave her a sandwich and some hugs.

One day, while talking with a group of women in Carol's apartment, I asked them about malnutrition. A family of four, say, one adult and three children, should receive the maximum of $366 in food stamps each month. "How can we not go hungry when we have to cash in our food stamps to pay the utility bills and buy nonfood items and wash our clothes?" asked Vanessa. "We have to sign our entire welfare check over to the landlord and still be short. The welfare check is $488 for a family of four or five and the rent is $500 to $550 a month. We wonder how the landlord feels taking our whole check and knowing that's all the family has." Families without cash for nonfood items know storekeepers who will give them $7 in cash for every $10 in food stamps. "But sometimes," says Carol, "we get lucky and find someone at the cash register who will combine the food and nonfood items, and take food stamps for both."

According to the New Jersey Commission on Hunger, there were roughly six hundred thousand hungry people in New Jersey in 1986. The commission identified "meager benefits provided by the state's social welfare system and housing costs" as the primary reason people did not have enough money for food. (A Legal Services attorney informed me that these figures have not been updated.)

In spite of all the problems, people living in the ghetto are not utterly without hope. Like most parents, people here try to keep up with holiday traditions, to take their children to church, and to teach them household responsibilities. The hope of Mary is to finish business school and get a job so that her two children will be able to live better than she did. "I want to give them a chance while they're young to have a good life. I'm not going to try and get them everything they want," she said, "just what they need."

"My kids are a trip," Carol laughed.

The other day while I am food shopping, my six-year-old, Kason, is bagging food for other people (there are no baggers). He will bag until the police officer comes and tell him to stop. It's considered hustling. But before he's stopped he usually make between three and five dollars. Yesterday he even told his nine-year-old sister what to do: "Keonda, come with me. I'll bag and you put the bags in the cart."

Discipline is really a problem. "Hardest of all right now," said Carol,

is teaching my ten-year-old daughter, Keisha, that she can't talk to me the way her friends talk to their parents. If she was living where they wear pink ribbons in their hair and say "may I," and "please" when they want to go somewhere, it would be easy. But her friends say, "I'm doing this! I'm going!" They don't ask. And she acts just like them. She puts that hand on her hip, puts her lip out and looks at me in that brazen way. I knocked that out of her fast.

Worrying about teenagers getting pregnant is another problem. "I'm not waitin' for my children to tell me about the urge," says Carol.

The first red spot I see in their panties, somebody gettin' the "vitamins." This is your "vitamin" and this is your "vitamin." That's it! They're on "vitamins" until they eighteen and they graduate high school and get a job. Until they get that diploma they gonna be takin' "vitamins."

I'm not encouraging that child to get pregnant. I'm protecting that child. These girls nowadays see welfare mothers with babies, they see their friends struggling. They don't want no baby. But yet they want to be with their boyfriends. And they think, "I'll just try—just one night."

Because parents are so overburdened with their struggle, often heavy responsibility falls on the children. Sometimes they must look after younger children and comfort adults who are sick or depressed as well. Recently, Carol went to the apartment down the hall and gave the children cereal and milk. She said,

> The house was a wreck. We washed out some bowls. The grandmother was on the bed and thanked me. She was paralyzed on one side after heart surgery. When I got back to my place, I cried. Kids shouldn't live like that. The mother loves the kids. She's young and uneducated. They don't know about three meals a day. They talk a lot about dinner. They think one meal. There's no breakfast or lunch. You can't tell them. They say, "You can't tell me what to do." But the child is the one who suffers.

"I tell them about 'No Frills' shopping," Carol continued,

> but they laugh at me because it's not Del Monte. They got to get that out of their head. They see the product on television and feel that's better. They already feel low class, so when they take their food stamps to buy things they saw on television they feel better about themselves. Even though they could save money on No Frills. How can I tell them how to compare, look at the weight and the price, not how pretty it's laid out? How to buy three boxes of something rather than one? It's the children who suffer in the end.

One day when I was in Carol's place, Mary asked her to call the ambulance (p. 57). "I'm so scared," she said. "I think I'm losing the baby." Mary is eighteen years old. She has two small children and has had three miscarriages. Even though she was in pain, she wanted to talk, to take her mind off her immediate problems.

Mary's husband was in jail. He had gone to buy a car on Friday and on the way home he went through an intersection and almost hit a police car. He had no registration or insurance with him. "In our neighborhood," she explained, "when you get locked up on Friday you don't see nothing until Monday morning. Nothing in the legal system works on weekends for us." As if to make matters worse, that morning the children wouldn't stop crying no matter what she did to appease them. Whatever toy she gave them, they threw it on the floor. She had to leave the apartment and go into the hall because she honestly thought she was going to hurt them. "I just couldn't take anymore," she said. "My nerves all came down this weekend. Now I have pains."

While waiting for the ambulance, I asked Mary about birth control. "Birth control!" she yelled.

> They won't tie my tubes until I'm older. I have a bad heart so I can't take the pill. I'm allergic to the foam. I can't be fitted for a diaphragm until I'm not pregnant for a while. My husband won't use a condom. Men in the ghetto say, "You're mine, why should I use a condom?" "Oh, you don't want no baby and you're sup-pose to be mine." And a woman catch their man with a condom in his wallet, she says, "What are you doin' with this? You got some kind of a problem?" Sex is a big part of our life.

All the women in Carol's place agreed. "It keeps us from moanin' all the time." Carol laughed.

Newark used to have a dynamic public school system, but it is now considered one of the worst in the state. The 1989–1990 dropout rate in Newark was 9.3 percent, which works out to be about 1,100 students. This reflects a multitude of problems encountered by the very poor and, from a different angle, those who would educate them. It also reflects the sharp contrast in per capita spending on schools in Newark compared to those in the surrounding suburbs. For example, Newark has only two-thirds as much to spend per pupil as Livingston, a nearby suburb. This means that Livingston can spend $100,000 more on a class of thirty than Newark. Central High School, one of the largest in the district, recently made a significant change in its dropout rate. Through an innovative program for rewarding teachers and students for good attendance, its dropout rate fell in one year from 21 percent to 8.9 percent.

Looking through the photographs I have taken in the Central

Learning

Ward, I am reminded again of the many problems that must be faced by those who live in poverty in order to get an education. For instance, Aida, whose family is from Puerto Rico, could hardly speak English. There was a large note written at the top of every school paper she brought home: "Aida needs help in English." Aida never smiled. Through various channels I found out that her school was supposed to provide special classes to help children improve their English and I mentioned this to her mother, who had just given birth to her seventh child. But with a new baby and no telephone, she probably didn't follow up on the information. When I went to visit one day, I found their door open and the apartment vacant. A neighbor said the family had been evicted, and she didn't know where they went.

Aida's situation was exactly what the 1968 New Jersey Governor's Commission on Civil Disorders had in mind when they recommended guided study halls for Spanish-speaking pupils. "These youngsters," the commissioners wrote, "have difficulty understanding their teachers, and can get little or no help at home from their Spanish-speaking parents, friends and relatives. Unless helped, they are bound to drop out of school."

Poorly educated or foreign-born parents often have difficulty helping their children get the most out of school. At the same time, there are success stories—like that of fifteen-year-old Omar, who just sort of appeared in front of my camera one day (p. 55). He used to live in the notorious "Hoodlum City," the Stella Wright housing project, but moved to Carol's building about two years ago. An honor student, with a mother dedicated to her children's success, he wants to be a lawyer and help all people.

Seldom does one "make it" without help. One such example appeared on the front page of the *Boston Globe* in 1991. A Vietnamese immigrant named Loe Tran, who came here in 1989 speaking no English, became his high school class valedictorian with the help of a devoted tutor. A Harvard undergraduate had become his "big brother" and worked intensively with him. "A drop in the bucket," said the mentor, adding, "there is a sea of black, white, Hispanic, and

Asian children who are in desperate need but will not be helped because we're practically the last act in town as services get cut more and more." Mentors and role models are what children from poorly functioning homes and poverty-stricken neighborhoods need most, according to many concerned observers.

One time, I decided to visit Omar's family in their third-floor apartment. I was curious to see what made him so different from many of the other teenagers in the area. Even though his mother, Maxine, didn't know I was coming, she greeted me warmly and invited me in without any hesitation. I told her that I was doing a book about the area and that I was impressed that Omar had received a college scholarship from the Ready Scholars Program. Anonymously funded, this program guarantees a college education to any child who stays in school. Now there are about a thousand Newark students enrolled.

Walking into the clean, uncluttered apartment, I thought about the differences between the people in the suburbs and here. Generally, suburbanites would hesitate to answer questions from a complete stranger. I have always been amazed at the ease with which people on low income answer questions. Once a sociologist friend of mine told me that this is because people in the ghetto are always being asked to explain themselves: to the welfare people, the landlord, the clinic, the food stamp people, the social workers, the police. Everywhere they turn, they must explain themselves. Otherwise, they could be shut off from services. So they don't have a strong sense of privacy. Also, they will jump at anything that seems like hope.

As we settled down on the couch, Maxine said, "I have taught my children how to survive. They can wash and iron their clothes. In fact, Omar can iron better than I can. They all know how to cook and clean up."

Maxine told me that her four children go to school clean and well fed. "If they say they're sick, they go straight to the clinic and get a note from the doctor," she said. "I keep them in the house with me. They have Nintendo games, television, books, and crayons. Omar is the oldest and I will help him no matter what it takes. I finished high school, but I never felt I was prepared for anything. My children will succeed. I told them if you don't know nothing, you don't go anywhere. Omar got *As* in first grade. He was always a good student."

Omar's mother continued with her story while the children stood around her. She gets child support, plus welfare, and her two-bedroom apartment costs $550 a month. She feels that it is relatively safe, but she must keep the windows by the fire escape locked at night no matter how hot it is. It would be a lot safer if the kids kept the front door downstairs locked and if the buzzer/intercom worked.

Many children are not as lucky as Maxine's. They don't have anyone able to encourage them. There are some who get most of their education from watching television, which, in many ways, is their only connection with the outside world.

I have seen children doing their homework on paper bags and telling me they want to be doctors. Helping the children with their homework can be quite a problem. Carol had told me that when she was drinking, she never helped her kids with homework. There wasn't any closeness or time spent together. Some parents say they "just don't understand" the school work their children bring home. They also talk about the energy it takes to survive each day, how crises totally occupy one's mind. In these circumstances the idea of teaching a child discipline, organizational skills, and motivational skills, much less becoming involved in any extracurricular activities, often seems like an impossible dream.

There are other problems as well; some of the material that the children are learning in the textbooks can seem remote to them and their parents. For example, Carol mentioned the word "hedge" as being unfamiliar to most of the children because they never saw a hedge. But ask the kids to explain a dirt hill or an empty lot, and they can tell you about that. Most of the words or stories have nothing to do with their everyday struggles. They may be in school that day only because their sister or brother had to stay home—there are not enough shoes to go around. Or their parents are too embarrassed to

dress them in outgrown or worn clothes. Or everyone overslept because the parents never got them up and dressed and fed them. Or
the children are exhausted from a night of crisis. Buildings burn-
ing down, people being shot. Police sirens, people shouting, robbers
breaking in. Rats. Being hungry, scared, and worried.

Some children seem to succeed in spite of it all, and then they
get sucked under. A straight-*A* student, Bob graduated from high
school at the head of his class. A year later, he joined his friends selling
dope. When other children see something like this happen, they tend
to become skeptical about adult assurances that hard work pays off.

The school system itself generates cynicism. "I don't understand
it," said Carol.

> If they are absent fifteen days they will keep you back—so the
> kids go to school sick and the nurse sends them home. But if
> they keep you back the first year they can't keep you back the
> second year—I don't understand that. Keisha is in the first
> grade—her test scored 1.0 in reading and they said that's not
> first grade reading. So she stayed back in the first grade last year.
>
> Now I know a kid that scored 0.9 and passed and Keisha
> scored 1.0 and failed—and she was a point higher than the kid
> next door. Then the school tell me that if she pass the score next
> year or not they got to pass her—'cause they can only keep her
> back one time in the same grade. She can stay out of school the
> second time for half a year and they still will pass her. Doesn't
> that make a lot of sense?
>
> I don't know what's wrong with the Board of Education. If she
> scores 1.0 this year she will pass—Newark is a trip—sounds
> like folks in the Board of Education ain't wrapped too tight. They
> ain't got the brains—this don't make no sense. Now Keonda just
> passed into the first grade and if she's out fifteen days she will
> stay back. If Keisha is out thirty days or whatever she will pass.
>
> What's even worse, they tell the children this stuff. So what
> you think about a child that stayed back in the eighth grade last

year? He don't worry about it. He ain't do nothin' this year because he know they gonna pass him. He gonna start ninth grade as dumb as a jackbird. What you gonna do?

Recently, Kason's third-grade teacher told Carol that he is the smartest child in the class. "How can that be?" said Carol. "He can't even read." "That's true," she said, "but the other thirty-five can't spell their names."

Transcending

The children in the Central Ward dream and play make-believe like children anywhere. Like squirrels, they tangle 'round and 'round on car hoods, beds, sidewalks, dirt lots, in the hallways, everywhere being tough and gentle, precise in each of their practiced movements. They want to be police officers or professional baseball or basketball players, lawyers, doctors, electrical engineers, nurses, artists, or soldiers.

The children are the source of my deepest joy, as well as my deepest sorrow. I still recall the feather-light hand of Danielle and her sorrowful expression as we walked up the stairs to the roof in order for me to photograph her. Or the gentleness of Jennifer, who never said a word, but stayed as long as I wanted, breaking my heart as I captured her faraway look. Only after photographing Aida for weeks, giving her books, her first doll, and pictures I had taken of her, did I see the slightest suggestion of a smile on her face.

Most of the children I work with are hungry. Hungry for food, for hugs and attention, for toys, or for paper and pencils in order to do their homework. They are thrilled to be photographed. And, like most children, they love being with their parents.

Despite the many health problems and the fatigue that come from living in this environment, exuberance and creativity are still alive. Rap songs are especially popular and have actually made their way into the mainstream. Youngsters spend hours creating songs that reflect their world.

I'm just a popcorn peanut
toy MC.
Now don't you never in your life
try to battle with me.
You're just a forest ranger
messin' with danger.
I don't know
you must be a stranger.
                                        —Jermaine, 16

In the suburbs the kids have drill teams, but there they wear tassels and skirts and hats with gold braid. The children in the Central Ward also have drill teams, without uniforms, "doing their little foot dances," said Carol. "But they have nasty words in their drill teams. Why? Because their environment is nasty. It's all they hear. I told my children they can't play no drill teams. Some of the words that I heard the children saying were, 'I wanna fight you,' 'I don't like you, gonna hurt you,' and as they went along somebody said something insulting about another child's house or family. The other one got mad. There was a fight."

Another game where money is not needed is basketball, played here with a plastic ball and a garbage can. Whoever sinks the ball in the can eleven times wins. But "flipping" gymnastics is the most popular (p. 40). I can hardly look as these children twist and twirl in midair, landing feet first on rocks, glass, and other debris. They practice on their beds or on the mattresses in the garbage, they flip off cars or dirt banks. Discarded mattresses are also used for playing house. "We're cooking for the hungry people," one group of children told me as they mixed up batches of flour and water.

Because of the access to certain sports, children in the ghetto sometimes become quite expert at what they do. Many professional players have come from the ghetto. But I doubt there will be many swimmers or skiers or tennis players or golfers. I was surprised one day when Omar, helping me take in bundles of clothes and food from my car, showed me the certificate he had just received for winning fourth place in the City Golf Tournament. "At first, I didn't like golf," he said, "but my friend said, 'Oh, come on, you might like it.' I started playing and I did like it. I practice at Weequahic Park. It's free and open to the public. I have my own golf clubs. The man who runs the golf course gave them to me because he said I play real good and he liked me very much."

The only playground close to this area is Ripple Field, an abandoned Board of Education property that many famous sports figures used while they were growing up. Now the children play among the dead animals, broken swings, and in the broken-down building that at one time was used for showers and locker rooms (pp. 34–35). At night the children watch from their windows as teenagers and grown-ups crash and burn stolen cars in the field, break bottles, fight, and use dope. It is from these same windows in the daytime that the adults watch their children play.

A block from Ripple Field is Sabbazz High School. Since they no longer use the field, the students are not allowed to leave the school at all during the day. For sports practice they are bused to Weequahic Park, even though directly across the street from the school is an empty lot, at least a city block long, where apartment buildings have burned and been demolished.

Stories are flying about the plans for this land. Most recently, a staff member from the Board of Education said that a stadium is projected so that the area will have a decent playground—not only for the youngsters, but also for the high school students. They would just have to cross the street and could enjoy being outside—practicing their sports, holding graduation and other ceremonies in a place they can identify with and call their own. Plus the city would not have to pay out the huge expense for buses.

"Not so," says Carol. "They'll never build a stadium. They're going to build middle-class housing on that land."

Children in the ghetto are enterprising. Here they have their own car wash. When they are allowed to open the fire hydrant, they hold a piece of wood in front of the gushing water. When a car passes with a driver who doesn't want it to be washed, he signals no. Then the children take the wood away and the water flows onto the street. But with an encouraging toot of the horn, or a gesture by the driver, the child raises the wood and the stream of water sprays the car. The car goes slowly through, turns around, and gets the opposite side watered down.

I suppose, though, that whatever transcending there is here doesn't last long. In the photographs of these children's faces you can see what's really happening in the ghetto.

The surface quality of a child's face does not always register on film in the same way it appears directly. Usually, when I look straight at Omar's face or even Danielle's, I just see regular kids living in a ghetto—animated and involved with each other. Until I get into my darkroom. There I see a deep sadness. The camera has picked up the tragedy. I believe that years of witnessing and experiencing horrors similar to those in war zones affects all children, regardless of their family situations.

Since this book was written Carol's and Rasheek's fathers have both died from strokes. Teddy was 57. Tino was 68. Carol's mother, Joyce, suffered multiple strokes and is now living in a nursing home, occasionally staying for an extended time with Carol. She still has not used her artificial leg.

In September 1993, Omar started college; he plans to become a pediatrician.

The father of Alicia's children was stabbed to death while taking a bath in a friend's house. Alicia found a reliable person to take care of her two children and went back to work.

Mary now lives in Carol's former basement apartment on Irvine Turner Boulevard. She was in the hospital recently with a collapsed lung.

While Margo was still pregnant, the baby was diagnosed as likely to have Down's syndrome. Margo chose not to have an abortion, and the baby, a boy, was born with no Down's syndrome.

Carol's son, Kason, now nine years old, is still struggling to read. He has been promoted to the fifth grade, even though he cannot read at a third-grade level. Carol's letter to the school strongly requesting that he be kept back has been ignored. His sister Keisha is a typical thirteen-year-old, to whom friends and clothes are important. She is now "on the vitamins."

Carol's eleven-year-old daughter, Keonda, and Angie's daughter have both been diagnosed as "mentally impaired."

Rasheek never heard from the sanitation job and is still waiting for any day work that comes along.

After waiting for over ten years, Carol finally received Section Eight housing approval in June 1993. Under Section Eight a person's rent is subsidized for apartments approved by HUD (Department of Housing and Urban Development). Once notified, Carol had sixty days to find an apartment; if she failed to find one, she would lose her voucher and go back on the waiting list.

For the first time in her life, Carol felt that she would finally have a choice about where she was going to live, and she was persistent in

◀ ◀ ◀

Carol's present apartment on Madison Avenue, Rasheek and Kason in doorway, Carol looking out the window, October 1993

her search for a suitable place. Over and over she found a good place, and everything would be going so well, she told me. The landlords seemed nice, the apartment was in good condition, and the area was safe. Then she would have to indicate her "employment" on the application form, and each time she wrote in "welfare" everything suddenly changed. The owners became distant and told her the apartment had "already been rented." "I hate writing in 'welfare,'" said Carol. "I can't wait until I'm off it."

As the sixty-day limit approached, Carol had to settle for a place, still in the Central Ward, rundown and unsafe but bigger than what she had (p. 138). The rent is $854 a month. Her landlord is *C* from Irvine Turner Boulevard, but now he fixes things for her, Carol says, because the government will shut off his rent check if he doesn't. The other tenants, however, who are not on Section Eight, have little luck getting their fallen ceilings fixed. "They don't see that man until rent day," says Carol. "That's when he leaves his rich home in Summit and visits us."

Carol received her high school diploma, with honors, in January 1994. Shortly before she graduated, Carol was called into her school principal's office and asked to sign her name as she would like it to appear on her diploma. "That was the most important thing I've ever signed for. It's like having a key to keep going." Because of new welfare regulations, Carol has been going to the Essex County College and Training, Incorporated, to study computerized office skills from 9 A.M. to 5 P.M. for six months. Her hope after this is to continue on at Essex County College to study social studies in human relations. Her dream is ultimately to be a teacher or a social worker.